PROPERTIES OF ECOSYSTEMS

1:1
answersingenesis
Petersburg, Kentucky, USA

ANSWERS IN GENESIS **SCIENCE** BY DEBBIE & RICHARD LAWRENCE

God's Design® for Chemistry & Ecology is a complete chemistry and ecology curriculum for grades 3–8. The books in this series are designed for use in the Christian school and homeschool, and provide easy-to-use lessons that will encourage children to see God's hand in everything around them.

First edition
Third printing: August 2010

Copyright © 2008 by Debbie and Richard Lawrence

ISBN: 1-60092-163-9

Cover design: Brandie Lucas
Layout: Diane King
Editors: Lori Jaworski, Gary Vaterlaus

Published by Answers in Genesis, 2800 Bullittsburg Church Rd., Petersburg KY 41080

Printed in China

www.answersingenesis.org • www.godsdesignscience.com

PHOTO CREDITS

TABLE OF CONTENTS

WELCOME TO
GOD'S DESIGN®
FOR CHEMISTRY & ECOLOGY

You are about to start an exciting series of lessons on chemistry and ecology. *God's Design® for Chemistry & Ecology* consists of three books: *Properties of Matter, Properties of Atoms and Molecules,* and *Properties of Ecosystems.* Each of these books will give you insight into how God designed and created our world and the universe in which we live.

No matter what grade you are in, third through eighth grade, you can use this book.

3rd–5th grade

Read the lesson and then do the activity in the ⬤ box (the worksheets will be provided by your teacher). After you complete the activity, test your understanding by answering the questions in the ⬛ box. Be sure to read the special features and do the final project.

6th–8th grade

Read the lesson and then do the activity in the ⬤ box. After you complete the activity, test your understanding by answering the questions in the ⬛ box. Also do the "Challenge" section in the ⬤ box. This part of the lesson will challenge you to do more advanced activities and learn additional interesting information. Be sure to read the special features and do the final project.

There are also unit quizzes and a final test to take.

Throughout this book you will see special icons like the one to the right. These icons tell you how the information in the lessons fit into the Seven C's of History: Creation, Corruption, Catastrophe, Confusion, Christ, Cross, Consummation. Your teacher will explain these to you.

When you truly understand how God has designed everything in our universe to work together, and how He is working out His plans, then you will enjoy the world around you even more. So let's get started!

UNIT

1

INTRODUCTION TO ECOSYSTEMS

WHAT IS AN ECOSYSTEM?

Biomes

How big is an ecosystem?

Words to know:

habitat

ecology

biosphere

biotic

abiotic

ecosystem

biome

flora

fauna

climate

Challenge words:

biogeographic realm

ecozone

Where do you live? You probably live in a house or an apartment with your family. Your home is in a neighborhood with other homes. The people who live around you are your neighbors. Your home and neighborhood make up your **habitat**; it is the environment in which you live. Animals and plants live in neighborhoods, too. The study of plants and animals and the environment in which they live is called **ecology**. In this book you are going to learn about many habitats and how the plants, animals, and other organisms in them interact.

The **biosphere** is the part of the earth that contains life. The biosphere includes the atmosphere, the surface of the earth, a small part of the crust of the earth, and the water that covers most of our planet. As we study ecology, we will be learning about the many different areas within the biosphere of earth. The earth is the only known planet that has a biosphere; it is the only planet that contains life. This life was created by God, and when He created life, He designed the earth so that things work together to allow life to continue.

The biosphere contains both biotic and abiotic things. **Biotic** describes things which are alive. Other things around us are **abiotic**, which means they are not alive. What kinds of things are biotic? Plants and animals make up the most visible of biotic organisms. Fungi, bacteria, and single-celled organisms are also biotic. What kinds of things are abiotic? Some non-living things include the minerals in the soil, water, chemicals, sunshine, and man-made objects. All of the living and non-living things in a particular area affect each other.

All of the biotic and abiotic items in a particular area make up an **ecosystem** and many ecosystems together make a **biome**. The plants in an ecosystem are called the **flora** of the ecosystem and the animals are called its **fauna**.

There are many different ecosystems in the world. The types of living things in an ecosystem are determined by many factors. The most important factor determining which plants and animals live in a certain area is the **climate**, which is the general or average weather conditions of a certain region, including the amount of sunlight the area receives, the average temperatures, and the amount of moisture available. Because the earth is tilted with respect to the sun, the amount of sunlight that an area receives depends on where you are located between the poles and the equator. The poles receive very little direct sunlight, whereas the equator receives a large amount of direct sunlight.

Ecosystems change as you move from the poles toward the equator. Ecosystems also change as you move from east to west across a continent. The terrain causes changes in the climate so the environments are varied in different locations. As you study the lessons in this book you will learn about the many wonderful ways that God created the life on our planet to interact with its environment. ■

A coral reef is an example of a marine ecosystem.

FUN FACT

The Greek word for habitat is *oikos*. The study of habitats is thus oekologie from which we get the work ecology. The word ecosystem is a shortened version of ecological system and the word biome is a shortened version of biological home.

MY BACKYARD HABITAT

Purpose: To become aware of different elements in your surroundings or habitat

Materials: string, yardstick/meter stick, "My Backyard Habitat" worksheet, magnifying glass

Procedure:

1. Although most animals live in the same habitat their whole lives, humans move about from one habitat to another. Make a list of all of the habitats you spend time in each week.

2. Closely examine the habitat in your backyard. Use string to mark out a square that is 1 yard (1 m) long on each side.

3. While standing up, carefully look at what is inside your square. Write your observations on a copy of the "My Backyard Habitat" worksheet.

4. Now, get down on your knees and use a magnifying glass to closely observe the smaller things in your square. Look for small animals, decaying plants, small twigs, paper, plastic, etc. Record all of your observations on your worksheet.

5. Listen to the sounds that can be heard from your square. Again record your observations.

6. Record the weather conditions on your worksheet.

7. List any ways that you think the animals that you observe use the other things that you have observed in your square.

8. Take photos of your area and what you found. Save your worksheet and your photos and include them in the notebook you are going to be making throughout this study.

Conclusion: Nothing can live in isolation. Even the smallest insect needs food and shelter and uses objects in its environment to provide these things. This in turn affects other animals and plants that are living in the area.

ECOZONES

As we study the different types of ecosystems we will see that some animals live only in certain parts of the world even though the climatic conditions in other parts of the world would support those animals. For example, zebras do not live on the great plains of North America even though the environment is very similar to the savannah in which they live in Africa. Another example is the many marsupials that live only in Australia. If conditions are right for these animals to live in other places, why are they only found in a particular area?

There are many different possible explanations, but one likely explanation is called the Ararat migration hypothesis. The Bible tells us that representatives from all of the land animals were saved from the Great Flood on Noah's Ark and that the Ark came to rest on the mountains of Ararat. Thus, all of the animals had to make their way from Ararat to the other parts of the world.

It is believed that after the Flood there was an Ice Age which created large ice sheets around the world. This lowered the water level and would have exposed land bridges between areas of the world that do not touch today. This would have allowed animals to migrate over the land into areas that are farther from Ararat, which is in modern Turkey. After several hundred years, the ice sheets began to melt, creating barriers that prevented further migration.

The natural barriers of large bodies of water, such as the oceans, as well as very high mountains or large deserts, keep many animals from migrating over large distances. Today, scientists recognize six major areas of land that are separated by one or more of these large barriers. These areas of land are called biogeographic realms or ecozones.

The *palearctic realm* is the area containing Eurasia and north Africa. It is isolated from other realms by oceans to the north, west, and east, and the Himalayan mountains and Sahara Desert to the south. Sub-Saharan Africa is part of the *afrotropical realm*, which is surrounded by oceans on the west, south, and east and the Sahara Desert on the north. The *Indo-Malay realm* is the area west and south of the Himalayan mountains and includes India and most of southeast Asia. Australia and the surrounding islands comprise the *Australian realm*. North America makes up the *Nearctic realm* and Central and South America comprise the *Neotropical realm*.

These realms are relatively isolated so the animals that live in one realm cannot easily move to another realm. On a copy of the World Map:

1. Label each of the following barriers:

   a. Atlantic, Pacific, Indian, Arctic, and Antarctic Oceans

   b. Sahara Desert

   c. Himalayan Mountains

2. Color each biogeographic realm a different color.

3. Create a key to label and identify each realm.

4. Save this map to add to the first section of your notebook.

GARDEN OF EDEN

THE FIRST ECOSYSTEM

As Adam walked along with Eve he reached up and grabbed a perfectly ripe fruit from the tree and offered it to Eve. "Hungry?"

"Yes, thank you." Eve took the fruit and bit into it as Adam reached up again and took one for himself.

The two walked on a little further as they thought about the conversation Adam had with God the night before. They both enjoyed their time with God and looked forward to it. God had given them everything they needed. The weather was always perfect, food was always just an arm's reach away, and even when they were separated from each other, God had provided animals of all kinds to keep them company. It was a perfect world—it was the Garden of Eden.

The Garden of Eden was the very first ecosystem. No one knows exactly what the Garden was like or where it was located; but we do know a few things based on what the Bible says. In Genesis 1, as God is making the universe, six times He says that what He made was "good." This meant without any flaws or defects. Genesis 1:31 says, "Then God saw everything that He had made, and indeed it was very good. So the evening and the morning were the sixth day."

All God made worked together perfectly and all was beautiful.

In chapter 2 we see a little more detail about the last day of creation:

> This is the history of the heavens and the earth when they were created, in the day that the LORD God made the earth and the heavens, before any plant of the field was in the earth and before any herb of the field had grown. For

the LORD God had not caused it to rain on the earth, and there was no man to till the ground; but a mist went up from the earth and watered the whole face of the ground. And the LORD God formed man of the dust of the ground, and breathed into his nostrils the breath of life; and man became a living being.

The LORD God planted a garden eastward in Eden, and there He put the man whom He had formed. And out of the ground the LORD God made every tree grow that is pleasant to the sight and good for food. The tree of life was also in the midst of the garden, and the tree of the knowledge of good and evil. …

Then the LORD God took the man and put him in the garden of Eden to tend and keep it. And the LORD God commanded the man, saying, 'Of every tree of the garden you may freely eat; but of the tree of the knowledge of good and evil you shall not eat, for in the day that you eat of it you shall surely die.'

And they were both naked, the man and his wife, and were not ashamed." (Genesis 2: 4–9, 15–17, 25)

From these passages we can learn a few things about the first ecosystem. God watered the plants by using a mist, which may have been a fog or a very fine rain. We know that man and animals could eat all the fruit that grew on the trees; both man and the animals ate only plants. Since man had not sinned yet there was no death of man or animals in the world. We know that all the trees and plants were very pleasing to look at. The insects that flew or crawled to pollinate the plants did not sting, bite, or bother Adam, Eve, or any of the animals. Man and all the animals lived in harmony with each other and with the plant life around them.

We can conclude from verse 25 that the weather was very mild. Adam and Eve had no need for clothing because they had not sinned. We can surmise from this that the temperatures were mild enough that they were not cold, even at night, without coverings.

The evidence of this mild tropical climate is not only found in the Bible but also in fossil records from around the world. Fossils show tropical plant life in almost every location on the globe. This shows that at one time much of the earth was warm and moist. Again, science agrees with God's Word.

So why and how did the earth change? Why do we have such extreme conditions now? Did man cause it? As we read in Genesis 3:17–18, after man sinned:

Then to Adam He said, "Because you have heeded the voice of your wife, and have eaten from the tree of which I commanded you, saying, 'You shall not eat of it':

"Cursed is the ground for your sake; in toil you shall eat of it all the days of your life. Both thorns and thistles it shall bring forth for you, and you shall eat the herb of the field."

From this passage we know that thorns and thistles are part of the curse; therefore, before man sinned the plants did not have thorns, and thistles did not grow. We can also see that God took away Adam's easy supply of food. Adam would now have to work for his food. Not only were Adam and Eve punished for their sin, the whole earth and universe were cursed because of it (see Romans 8:20–22). This means that not only did man lose his ready supply of food and have to work for it, but the curse on the earth applied to all the animals, plants, and all living things. Now they too would have to struggle to survive.

Many of the things you will learn about in the following lessons did not apply to the original creation. You will learn about competition, food chains, overpopulation, and extinction. These are a result of the curse brought on by man's sin. In the original ecosystem there were no predators and prey because there was no death. However, even though the world we have today is cursed, it is still a magnificent place to live. Even though the original perfection is gone, the mark of the Creator remains and can still declare His glory.

NICHES

What's your job?

LESSON

2

What is a niche?

Words to know:

niche

population

community

No organism lives by itself. All plants and animals are interconnected in one way or another. For example, a flower growing in a garden cannot reproduce without a bee or other insect to pollinate its flowers. The bee must have nectar to eat and to make honey. Other animals and humans eat the honey made by the bee. They are all connected to each other. Each plant and each animal in an ecosystem has a particular role to fill or a job to do. The job or role that a particular organism performs is called its **niche**.

An animal's niche is determined by many factors. It is determined by what it eats and what eats it. An animal may eat only particular plants, but may be eaten by several other animals in the area, thus its niche includes eating plants and providing food for other animals. How the animal acts and what it does help to determine its niche as well. The animal may also play a role in spreading disease or in providing waste to help plants to grow. All of these things, and many more, help determine what niche an animal will fill.

Similarly, plants can fill different niches as well. We usually think of plants in terms of the animals that eat them. But plants also provide shelter and homes for many organisms. Animals can use plants in many different ways. Also, plants may compete with other plants. All of these things affect the niche that a particular plant fills.

The **population** of a particular species of plant or animal is determined by the number of individuals of that species in a particular area. All of the different populations living together in an area make up a **community**. The size of populations and the particular types of populations in a community also affect the niche that each animal and plant fills within that community.

Niche can refer to two different kinds of roles. As we have described it so

AN EARTHWORM'S NICHE

Purpose: To observe an earthworm's niche by making an environment for it to live in

Materials: jar, dark soil, sand, oats, earthworms, dark construction paper, tape

Procedure:

1. Fill a jar ¼ of the way with moist, dark soil. Add a layer of lighter colored sand then another layer of soil.

2. Sprinkle 2 tablespoons of oats on top of the soil.

3. Add 10–12 earthworms to the jar then seal the jar. Punch holes in the lid to allow air into the jar.

4. Wrap a piece of dark construction paper around the jar and tape it in place. Put the jar in a cool location out of direct sunlight.

5. Observe your earthworm habitat each day for several days by removing the paper and looking at the contents of the jar. What do you see happening inside the jar?

6. Take photos of your earthworm habitat each day and include them in your notebook.

Conclusion:

After several days, you should observe the different colors of soil mixing together. This is one of the important niches filled by earthworms; they help to break up and mix soil to make it more fertile.

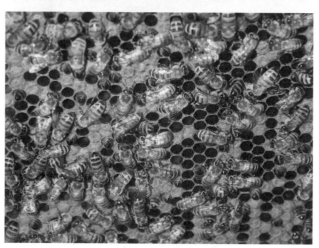

Different bees have different niches within their colony.

far, an animal's niche is the role that it plays in the community—the job that it does in its neighborhood. But niche can also refer to the role that the animal plays within its family or population. For example, a bee's niche within its environment is as a pollinator and as a producer of honey. But within the colony of bees, different bees play different roles. Sterile female bees are the workers that gather the nectar and make the honey. The queen bee is the only one that produces eggs for reproduction. The male bees, called drones, are responsible to fertilize the eggs. Thus different bees have different niches within their colony. ■

WHAT DID WE LEARN?

- What is a niche?
- Name two factors that determine an animal's niche.
- What is a population?
- What is a community?
- What are two different kinds of niches an animal can have?

TAKING IT FURTHER

- What different niches do you fill in your family and in your community?
- How does competition for food and other resources affect the niche of a plant or animal?

SETTING UP YOUR NOTEBOOK

Purpose: To build a notebook, recording all of the things you learn about ecosystems. Today, you are going to start your notebook by making dividers for each section of your book.

Materials: 3-ring binder, nine dividers for the notebook

Procedure:

1. Obtain a 3-ring binder.

2. Make nine dividers for your notebook. Label the dividers as follows:

   a. Introduction

   b. Grasslands

   c. Forests

   d. Aquatic ecosystems

   e. Tundra

   f. Deserts

   g. Mountains

   h. Animal behaviors

   i. Ecology

3. Add your photos and worksheet from lessons 1 and 2 to the first section of your notebook.

Conclusion:

As you complete each activity in this book, add your worksheets, reports, photos, etc. to your book. When you have completed the study of ecosystems you will have the book to help you remember what you learned.

WHAT'S MY NICHE?

On a piece of paper, describe the niche occupied by each of the following plants or animals. Be sure to include all the possible uses and different areas where you might find them. Include your list in your notebook.

Tree

Wolf

Mouse

Robin

Grass

FOOD CHAINS

Does it have links?

LESSON

3

What is a food chain?

Words to know:

food chain

producer

consumer

herbivore

carnivore

omnivore

food web

Challenge words:

carrying capacity

All organisms in a biome are connected to each other in various ways. The primary connection between these living things is the flow of energy. The flow of energy from one organism to another is called a food chain. Another way to think of a **food chain** is: a series of organisms in the order that they feed on one another.

Nearly all food chains begin with green plants. Green plants change the energy of the sun into food, primarily glucose (a type of sugar), through the process of photosynthesis. These plants are called **producers**. Any organism that does not produce its own food, but instead eats plants or other animals, is called a **consumer**. A first order, or primary, consumer is the animal that eats the plant. The second order, or secondary, consumer is the animal that eats the first order consumer, and so on. Most food chains have three or four levels; only a few food chains have more than five levels.

Animals that eat only plants are primary consumers and are called **herbivores**. All animals were herbivores in God's original creation (Genesis 1:29–30). Most grazing animals such as deer, antelope, cows, and horses are herbivores. Animals that eat only other animals are secondary consumers and are called **carnivores**. Animals did not start eating other animals until after the Fall of man. Some common carnivores include wolves, lions, and snakes. Some animals eat both plants and animals and are called **omnivores**. Black bears are omnivores. They will eat berries and honey, as well as fish and other animals.

A common food chain might start with acorns from an oak tree which are eaten by a squirrel. The squirrel might then be eaten by an owl. In this food chain, the oak tree is the producer, the squirrel is the primary consumer, and the owl is the secondary consumer. Another food chain might begin with corn which is eaten by a mouse. The mouse is then eaten by a weasel which is eaten by a wolf. This food chain has four levels.

Many animals eat more than one kind of food and many animals have more than one predator; therefore, there can be multiple food chains containing the same plants and animals. The interactions among multiple food chains is called a **food web**. It is called a web because when arrows are drawn showing all of the possible ways that energy flows through the various animals, it resembles a spider's web. ■

FUN FACT

Before the Fall of man, all animals and people were herbivores (Genesis 1:29–30). After the Flood, God allowed people to eat animals as well as plants (Genesis 9:3).

FOOD CHAINS & WEBS

Draw a picture of a food chain. You can make up your own or use the plants and animals listed below; they are not in the correct order. Draw arrows in the direction that the energy is flowing.

Grass   Hawk
Snake   Grasshopper
Frog

On your drawing, identify the producer, 1st order consumer, 2nd order consumer, 3rd order consumer, and 4th order consumer.

Draw a food web. Again, you can make up your own or use the organisms listed below. Make sure the arrows show the flow of energy in the web.

Mosquito   Deer
Robin   Grass
Flowers   Wolf
Fox   Butterfly
Toad

Add these drawings to your notebook.

WHAT DID WE LEARN?

- What is a food chain?
- What is a producer?
- What is a consumer?
- What is a food web?
- List two herbivores.
- List two carnivores.
- List two omnivores.

TAKING IT FURTHER

- Is a black bear a first or second order consumer?
- Is man an herbivore, carnivore, or omnivore?
- Explain how a food chain shows energy flow.

CARRYING CAPACITY

It is important to understand how the various organisms in a particular area fit together in a food chain or a food web. This helps us to understand how many of a particular animal or plant can survive in that area. The number of a particular species in a given area is called the population. For example, if you counted all of the foxes living in a particular square mile area, that would be the fox population of that area.

The population of a particular species depends on many things. What things do you think affect the population? The amount of food available is a very important factor in determining how many of a species can survive. Population is also affected by how much space is available and how many other animals are competing for the same space and food. The population also depends on how many predators are living in the same area. Weather can also play a role in population. When the weather is mild, the animals and plants survive better than when the weather is unusually harsh.

The maximum population an area can support is called its carrying capacity. The carrying capacity of an area may vary from year to year depending on the weather. In years where growing conditions are good, such as years when there is adequate water and sunshine,

the plants grow well. This provides more food for the consumers, and the carrying capacity of the area increases. During times of drought, there are fewer plants so the carrying capacity of the area decreases.

As long as the population of a species is lower than the carrying capacity, the population may increase. When there is an adequate food supply the birth rate usually increases and the death rate decreases. This increases the population. However, when the population becomes larger than the carrying capacity, food becomes scarce so the death rate increases and the birth rate decreases. This causes the population to decrease.

We have shown how weather can change the carrying capacity of an area. What other factors can you think of that can affect the

carrying capacity of an area? For example, what would happen if a disease suddenly struck a prairie dog colony and killed a significant portion of the prairie dogs? This would decrease the food supply for all of the animals in the food web that eat prairie dogs, causing many of them to die, or to become weak because of lack of food. This would mean that the carrying capacity of the area was decreased.

Human activity can also greatly change the carrying capacity of an area. People can grow much more food in a given area than would naturally grow there. This means that more cattle can be fed from a given area when humans are growing the food. In general, when talking about populations and carrying capacity, scientists usually refer to conditions that have not been changed by human activity.

SCAVENGERS & DECOMPOSERS

Breaking it down

Why are scavengers important?

Words to know:

scavenger

decomposer

decomposition

law of conservation of mass

Food chains and food webs do not end when a plant or animal dies. The dead plant or animal still has a considerable amount of energy tied up in its tissues and cells. Fortunately, God created many different types of organisms that eat dead plants and animals. Some of these organisms eat the dead plants or animals and use the energy for their own survival. These types of organisms are called **scavengers**. Some examples of scavengers include vultures, flies, and earthworms. Many other animals are scavengers when given the opportunity, but may also hunt or eat live plants and animals as well. Lions are an example of an animal that will hunt when necessary, but will eat dead animals if they are available.

At the very end of every food chain are the **decomposers**. These are organisms that eat dead plant and animal material and break it down into basic elements and molecules such as nitrogen, carbon, and phosphorus. This process frees up those elements so they can be reused to grow new plants and provide food for new animals. The most common decomposers are bacteria and fungi. Bacteria and fungi

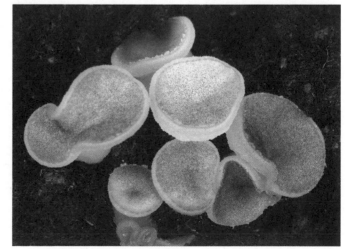

Fungi like these yellow fairy cups help decompose plant and animal material.

ADDING DECOMPOSERS

Add scavengers and decomposers to your food chain and food web pictures in your notebook.

also decompose animal waste to free up the materials that have been excreted.

The process of **decomposition** is a vital function. Without decomposition, all of the elements necessary for plant and animal life would become tied up in dead plants and animals and new plants and animals could not exist. The **law of conservation of mass** states that matter cannot be created or destroyed by any natural means, it can only change form. There is a limited amount of nitrogen, oxygen, carbon, and all other atoms in the world. This is why God created the world to recycle these materials. Decomposition is one way that these elements are recycled. ■

FUN FACT

Although many animals convert only about 10% of the food they eat into body mass, some animals are more efficient. Pigs convert about 20% of what they eat into body mass and turkeys convert as much as 30% of the energy they eat into body mass. This means that it takes less food to grow a pound of pork or turkey than it does to grow a pound of beef. Compare the prices of pork and turkey to the price of beef the next time you are at the store and see which meats are the most and least expensive.

WHAT DID WE LEARN?

- What are organisms called that eat dead plants and animals?
- Name two different animals that eat dead plants or animals.
- What types of organisms are at the end of every food chain?
- Name two common organisms responsible for decomposition.

TAKING IT FURTHER

- Why is decomposition so important?
- What physical law makes decomposition necessary?

POPULATION PYRAMIDS

In the previous lesson you learned that the population of a species depends on the amount of food available. Take a minute to think about how much grass a deer eats each day. Think about how many mice an owl must eat each night. In a healthy ecosystem would you expect to find more grass plants than deer? Of course, otherwise the deer would starve to death.

There must be significantly more producers in an area than consumers for life to continue. Similarly, there must be a significantly higher number of first order consumers than second order consumers in any particular area. For example, there may be hundreds of mice living in a field, but only one hawk living in the area. This is another way of talking about carrying capacity of an area.

In the same ecosystem the carrying capacity for one species will be very different from the carrying capacity for another species. If we were to draw a picture of the population of each species in a food chain it would resemble a pyramid. The plants would be the wide base at the bottom. The first order consumers would be a smaller number stacked on top of the producers. The second order consumers would be an even smaller number stacked on top of the first order consumers, and so on.

Although the numbers of first order consumers compared to the numbers of second order consumers varies greatly between different species, there is a rule called the 10% rule that is a good estimate of the relative populations that an area can support. On average an animal converts only about 10% of the energy it eats into body mass; the other 90% of the energy is used for searching for food, chewing, maintaining body functions, heating the body, and so forth. So there must be

at least 10 times as many first order consumers as second order consumers. Thus if an area can support 500 grasshoppers, it can support about 50 frogs and about 5 snakes.

Even though we said that producers/plants are at the bottom of the population pyramid, there is one group of organisms that is even more numerous than the producers. That group is the decomposers. Since decomposers are so small and must break apart every plant and animal after it dies, there are millions of bacteria for each plant or animal in a given area. Decomposers should actually be the base (largest part) of our pyramid.

Draw a population pyramid for each of the food chains that you drew in lesson 3. Don't forget to put decomposers at the bottom of the pyramid. Include these drawings in your notebook.

RELATIONSHIPS AMONG LIVING THINGS

Depending on each other

LESSON 5

How are organisms connected?

Words to know:

symbiosis

mutualism

predator

prey

parasitism

commensalism

epiphyte

competition

neutralism

The plants and animals in an ecosystem are connected in a variety of ways. In previous lessons you learned about food chains and food webs, which show the flow of energy from one organism to another. However, there are many other relationships between plants and animals besides the flow of energy. Any relationship between two different species living in close connection is called **symbiosis**.

There are several different types of symbiosis. The relationship most often associated with symbiosis is a relationship in which both organisms benefit. This is called **mutualism**. There are examples of mutualism all around us. You have a certain type of bacteria living in your digestive system, which helps you digest your food. This relationship provides a source of energy for the bacteria and for you, so you both benefit. Another example of mutualism is between the crocodile bird and the crocodile. Bits of food often get stuck between a crocodile's teeth. But he cannot brush and floss to get rid of it. Instead, the crocodile will open its mouth and the crocodile bird will land in the crocodile's mouth and pick out the food stuck between his teeth. Although the crocodile could just snap its mouth shut, the crocodile does not eat the bird. The bird gains a meal and the crocodile gains better dental health. In another example, the oxtail bird eats ticks and fleas off of the back of the rhinoceros. This feeds the bird and gets rid of pests for the rhino, as shown above.

Not all relationships between species are beneficial. Obviously the predator-prey relationship is beneficial for the **predator** (the hunter) but deadly for the **prey** (the hunted). Another type of relationship in which one species benefits and the other is harmed is **parasitism**. A parasite feeds off of another species causing harm, but usually not death, to the host. Common examples of parasites include lice, fleas, and many types of worms. These animals usually suck blood or live in the intestines of the host animal, which harms the host in a number of ways. There are parasitic plants as well as parasitic animals. Parasitic plants usually send a shoot into the roots or stems of another plant and steal some of the sap from the host plant.

A third type of symbiosis is **commensalism**. Like a parasite, the guest species benefits in some say from the host; however, the host is not harmed or benefited by the guest. One example of commensalism is the relationship between an epiphyte and a tree. In rainforests as well as other forests, the trees often become large enough to block most of the sunlight from reaching the forest floor. Many species of plants attach themselves to the bark of a tree at a height where the sunlight will reach them. These plants are called **epiphytes**. The attachment benefits the plant, but does not harm the tree. Another example of commensalism is the relationship between the remora and the shark. The remora is a fish that attaches itself to large aquatic animals such as sharks. The remora has a dorsal fin shaped like a suction cup. It attaches itself to the host by this suction cup and hitches a ride. The fish is also believed to eat leftovers that are dropped by the host during feeding. Thus the remora is benefited and the shark is not harmed.

Competition is another relationship between species. When two different species both eat the same food, they will compete for the limited resources in the area. Both species will be hurt by this competition if their populations become too large and there is not enough food for everyone. There can also be competition for space,

UNDERSTANDING SYMBIOSIS

Complete the "Symbiosis" worksheet.

Optional Activity:

Use a magnifying glass to examine a rock with a lichen on it. Lichens demonstrate a symbiotic relationship between fungi and green algae. The algae perform photosynthesis, which provides food for both organisms, while the fungi provide protection from the weather. This is a type of mutualism.

sunlight, and nutrients between various plant and animal species.

The final relationship between species is neutralism. **Neutralism** is the relationship where neither species benefits and neither is harmed. Many species do not eat each other and do not compete for the same resources so they coexist without much direct effect on each other. ■

WHAT DID WE LEARN?

- What is symbiosis?

- What is mutualism?

- What happens to each species in a parasitic relationship?

- Which species benefits in commensalism?

- What is competition among species?

- What is the name of a relationship in which neither species benefits nor is harmed?

TAKING IT FURTHER

- Why is competition considered harmful for both species?

- Explain how competition could keep the species from becoming too populated.

LIVER FLUKES

The liver fluke is a flatworm that has a very complex life cycle involving several different relationships with different animals. Research the life cycle of the liver fluke and make a chart showing each step. Label the different relationships that exist between the fluke and its various hosts.

Add your chart to your notebook.

OXYGEN & WATER CYCLES

What comes around goes around

LESSON

6

How are materials recycled?

Words to know:

photosynthesis

respiration

oxygen cycle

water cycle

Challenge words:

nitrogen cycle

The law of conservation of mass requires that all elements be conserved or recycled since no new matter can be made by any natural processes. We already talked about how decomposers break down the tissues of dead plants and animals to release the nitrogen, carbon, and other elements in them to be used again in new plants and animals. God has also established several other systems that recycle precious materials.

One of the most amazing demonstrations of the conservation of mass is the relationship between plants and animals. During **photosynthesis** plants utilize water and carbon dioxide, both of which contain oxygen atoms, to capture the energy of the sun as they rearrange these molecules to make sugar and oxygen. Animals then breathe in the oxygen and eat the sugar. During **respiration** the animals use the oxygen to break apart the sugar molecules to release the energy and in the process they release water and carbon dioxide back into the air, which can be reused by plants. This process is called the **oxygen cycle**. It not only demonstrates how the molecules are recycled, but also shows God's amazing plan for providing energy for all living things.

The oxygen cycle occurs in the water as well as in the air. As water flows, oxygen becomes dissolved in the water. Algae and plants growing in the water perform photosynthesis and release oxygen into the air and the water. Animals that live in the water absorb the oxygen from the water and use it to break down food. This creates carbon dioxide, which is released into the water and into the air where the plants and algae can absorb it and use it in photosynthesis.

Another important recycling process is the **water cycle**. Like all other materials, water must be used over and over again. We have already seen that water is recycled in the oxygen cycle as it is absorbed by plants and released by animals.

DEMONSTRATING THE WATER CYCLE

Purpose: To demonstrate the water cycle in your very own living room

Materials: potting soil, glass jar with lid, grass or other plant, camera or drawing materials

Procedure:

1. Place 2–3 inches of potting soil in the bottom of a glass jar.

2. Dig up a clump of grass, being sure to get as much of the roots as possible. Plant the grass in the jar.

3. Add enough water to moisten the soil, but don't make it soggy.

4. Tightly seal the jar with a lid.

5. Place the jar in a warm location and observe it several times a day for one week.

6. Take several pictures of your jar, showing the different stages of the water cycle. Use these pictures to make a water cycle poster to include in your notebook. If you don't have access to a camera, you can draw pictures of what you observe.

Questions:

• What do you observe happening in the jar?

• Does it look the same in the morning as it does in the afternoon?

Conclusion:

You should notice some fogginess or cloudiness in the jar as it warms up. As it cools you may notice water condensing on the sides of the jar. You should also notice that at other times the water is gone. This is the water cycle at work. Water is absorbed by the grass and some of it is used for photosynthesis and some of it is released into the air. Also, as the plant grows it breaks down some of the food it produces the same way that animals break down food. This process also releases water.

As the sun warms the inside of the jar, water also evaporates into the air. This can cause the inside of the jar to appear foggy. Later, as the air cools, the water condenses and falls back into the soil.

But water is recycled in other ways as well. Water in the world's oceans and lakes evaporates into the air when the sun warms the surface of the water. This water vapor moves through the atmosphere. As it cools it condenses and forms clouds. Eventually, the water becomes heavier than the atmosphere can support and falls back to the earth as precipitation. Some of this water is used by plants and animals while some of it flows back into the lakes and oceans. Thus, the water is constantly being recycled.

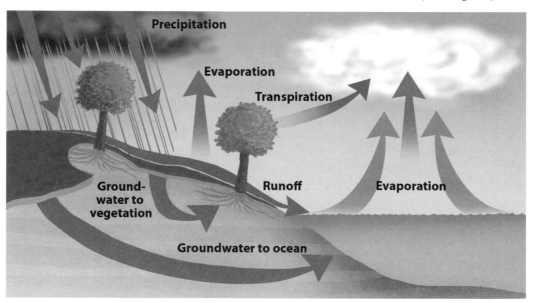

When you think about how well everything works together in our world, you have to stop and thank our Creator, God, who made it all! ■

WHAT DID WE LEARN?

- How do photosynthesis and respiration demonstrate the oxygen cycle?

- What are the major steps in the water cycle?

TAKING IT FURTHER

- Water exists in three forms: solid, liquid and gas. What phase is the water in before and after evaporation?

- What phase is the water in before and after condensation?

- What phase is the water in before and after precipitation?

NITROGEN CYCLE

Another important cycle that exists in nature is the nitrogen cycle. Nitrogen is a very important element needed to form amino acids and proteins, which are the building blocks of all plants and animals. Plants absorb most of their nitrogen from the soil and animals get nitrogen by eating plants. Most of this nitrogen eventually returns to the soil when decomposers break down the tissues of dead plants and animals.

Although the largest supply of nitrogen is in the atmosphere, plants cannot absorb nitrogen in this form. Nitrogen must be converted into nitrates that the plants can use. This is done in several ways. Some nitrogen gas is changed into a form useful to plants by lightning strikes. Other nitrogen gas is converted by nitrogen-fixing bacteria.

This is just a short overview of the nitrogen cycle. Do some research of your own to learn more about the nitrogen cycle. Then use what

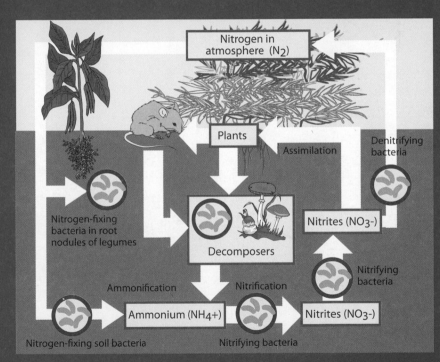

you have learned to write clues for the following words and create your own crossword puzzle. Add your puzzle to your notebook.

- Ammonia
- Nitrite
- Nitrate
- Bacteria

- Legumes
- Lightning
- Protein
- Fixation
- Roots
- Fertilizer
- Nitrification
- Decomposition

UNIT 2

GRASSLANDS & FORESTS

PROPERTIES OF

Biomes around the World

Where are they located?

LESSON

7

How are biomes distributed?

Words to know:

tropical zone

northern temperate zone

southern temperate zone

northern polar region

southern polar region

Challenge words:

ecotone

succession

pioneer plant

climax ecosystem

An ecosystem is all of the living and nonliving things that interact in a given area. From this perspective, a puddle of water could be considered an ecosystem. Similarly the whole earth could also be considered an ecosystem because every living thing on earth is connected in some way to every other living thing on earth. However, when scientists talk about biomes they usually mean a large region with a particular climate and the plants and animals that live in that region.

Areas that are very dry are called deserts. A desert is one type of biome. Another type of biome is the Arctic tundra, which is an area that is consistently cold and has a relatively short growing season. Other biomes include temperate forests and tropical forests. There are also various water biomes such as lakes and oceans. We will be studying each of these biomes as well as many others in the following lessons.

The earth is tilted with respect to the sun. So as the earth revolves around the sun the amount of sunlight reaching various parts of the earth is different. This is one of the most important factors contributing to the different climates around the world. The earth can be divided into five zones based on the amount of sunlight received. The **tropical zone** is the section of the earth located between the Tropic of Cancer (23.5° north latitude) and the Tropic of Capricorn (23.5° south latitude). This area centered around the equator receives the most direct sunlight all year round. Tropical biomes are located in this tropical zone.

Between the Tropic of Cancer and the Arctic Circle (66.5° north latitude) is the **northern temperate zone** and between the Tropic of Capricorn and the Antarctic Circle (66.5° south latitude) is the

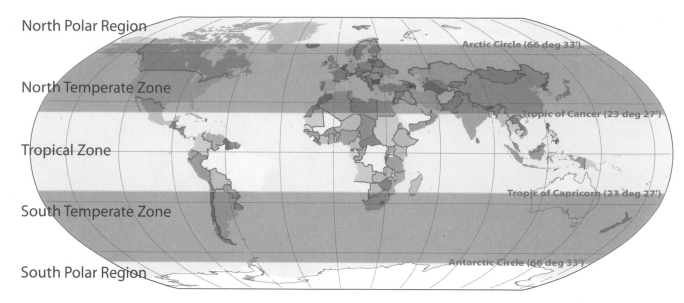

North Polar Region

North Temperate Zone

Tropical Zone

South Temperate Zone

South Polar Region

Arctic Circle (66 deg 33')

Tropic of Cancer (23 deg 27')

Tropic of Capricorn (23 deg 27')

Antarctic Circle (66 deg 33')

southern temperate zone. These zones receive more hours of sunlight in the summer and fewer hours of sunlight in the winter months than the tropic zone does. The temperate forests and grassland biomes are generally found in these zones.

North of the Arctic Circle is the **northern polar region** and south of the Antarctic Circle is the **southern polar region.** The polar regions are usually colder than the temperate regions and although they receive many hours of sunlight in the summer,

LOCATING BIOMES

Purpose: To become acquainted with the location of various biomes and to demonstrate how climate affects them

Materials: world atlas showing temperature and rainfall for the world as well as location of various biomes, three copies of the blank world map

Procedure:

1. Label one copy of the world map "Average Rainfall." Then color the map to indicate the annual average rainfall in each part of the world. Use a different color for each unit of rain, such as light blue for less than 10 inches of rain per year, dark blue for 10–20 inches of rain,

etc. Be sure to make a key for your map.

2. Label a second copy of the world map "Average Temperature." Your atlas may give average summer temperatures and average winter temperatures. If this is the case, make two maps. Again use different colors for different temperature bands. Make a key for your map.

3. Label the final copy of the world map "Biomes of the World." Use a different color for each biome. Be sure to include deserts, grasslands, mountains, oceans, tropical forests, temperate forests, and polar biomes on your map. Your atlas may show

other biomes as well which you may wish to include. Be sure to make a key for your map.

4. Place your maps side by side and compare the temperature and rainfall maps with the location of the various biomes. You should notice that polar tundra occurs in the polar regions where the temperatures are colder than other areas. You should also notice that there is a correlation to rainfall and the location of the deserts.

5. Place these maps in your notebook and use them to locate the various biomes as we study them in the following lessons.

the sunlight strikes the earth at a steep angle in these areas and much of the sunlight reflects off of the atmosphere and snow. Thus these areas remain fairly cool even in the summer time. You will find the Arctic tundra located in the polar regions.

As you study each biome, pay attention to where they are located around the world. ■

WHAT DID WE LEARN?

- Where is the tropical zone located?
- Where is the northern temperate zone located?
- Where is the southern temperate zone located?
- Where are the polar regions located?

TAKING IT FURTHER

- Why are the polar regions generally colder than the tropical regions even though they receive many more hours of sunlight each day during the summer?
- What correlations do you see between the temperature and rainfall maps that you made?

SUCCESSION

Although we will be studying several distinct ecosystems, in reality you don't just step from one ecosystem into another. There is generally an area between two different ecosystems which is a transitional area. This transitional area between two ecosystems is called an ecotone. It may contain plants and animals that are found in both ecosystems. For example, between a grassland and a forest you may find an area that has more trees than the grassland, but not enough trees to be considered a forest. Some animals are primarily found in the grasslands and others are primarily found in the forest, but in the ecotone between the two you may find animals living together that do not live together in either the grassland or the forest. You may also find animals

living in the ecotone that do not inhabit either of the bordering ecosystems.

Many ecosystems are fairly stable. They have the same types of plants and animals living there from year to year. However, some parts of ecosystems change over time. This change from one ecosystem to another is called succession. Succession occurs because the conditions in the ecosystem change. This change can be a slow change because of a changing climate, or it can be a sudden change because of a natural disaster such as a forest fire or flood, or it can be a change brought about because of the actions of people, such as the clearing of a field.

An area that is experiencing succession changes over time as different plants become dominant. Some plants can grow in harsh

conditions, but as these plants become more numerous, they change the environment, making it more attractive to different kinds of plants. These new plants then choke out the first plants, further changing the growing conditions. As the dominant plant species change, the dominant animal species will change as well.

The easiest way to understand succession is to think about an area of land that has experienced a sudden change. Let's think about a piece of land near the edge of a forest that has been cleared of all plants by a farmer. If the farmer does not plant crops, but instead just leaves the field alone, it will go through a series of changes over the years.

The first plants to move into an area after a change are called pioneer plants. These pioneers are usually plants that do not compete well with other plants, but which can reproduce more quickly than other plants. In our cleared field we will likely see mosses and small flowering plants such as dandelions grow up. These plants will attract small insects. As these pioneers become more numerous, they help to keep the water from evaporating and they add humus to the soil. This allows plants that grow more slowly to begin to grow. These plants may include grasses, ferns, and small shrubs. These new plants attract small mammals such as rabbits and mice to the area.

After many years, sun tolerant trees such as cottonwoods and chokecherries begin to grow. These plants provide more shade and cause some of the smaller plants to die out. At the same time, these larger plants attract larger animals including many birds and deer. Over the years, other successions will occur until the land returns to the ecosystem that originally occupied the land. This final, stable ecosystem is called the climax ecosystem.

Evolutionists have theorized that the earliest plant and animal species evolved into more

complex species over millions of years. Although at first glance succession may seem to support the evolutionary ideas, there are significant differences between what we observe in succession and what supposedly happens in evolution. Evolution says that the simple plants such as moss evolved and changed into more complex plants such as grass and other flowering plants. However, what we actually observe is that moss is replaced by flowering plants as seeds that blow in or are carried in by animals take root and grow. The moss does not change into a different species.

When moss is the dominant plant the dominant organisms are bacteria, but as grasses take over, worms and other small invertebrates move in. Evolutionists claim that bacteria evolved into worms, but we see that the animals are attracted by the available plant life and move in as new plants become available. The worms and other species already existed in other ecosystems and did not develop from the bacteria. Thus, what we actually observe in succession is very different from the supposed evolutionary processes described by some scientists.

Activity:

Research ecological succession on the Internet or in other sources.

Then make a poster showing the same area of land in various stages of succession. Possible ideas include bare rock to forest succession after

a volcanic eruption, aquatic succession, or succession after a forest fire or flood. Add this poster to your notebook.

Special FEATURE

ALEXANDER VON HUMBOLDT

1769–1859

Explorer, ecologist, meteorologist, government consultant, mining expert. All of these describe Alexander von Humboldt during his lifetime, but he is most remembered as being the father of ecology and the father of geography. He was born in Berlin, Germany in 1769 to an army major who served under Frederick the Great. When he was nine his father died leaving him and his older bother to be raised by their mother. She was said to be unemotional and showed little love to her boys. But she wanted the best for her children in education, and the wealth of the family made this possible. She had them tutored at home, and wanted both of them to enter either the military or civil service. Both of them had an aptitude for learning and their studies pointed them toward civil service.

Alexander attended several universities in Germany, always adding to his understanding of science, concentrating in geology and biology. When he was 22 he met the scientific illustrator who worked for Captain James Cook on his second voyage. The two hiked around Europe together. Humboldt later went to the Freiberg Academy of Mines and after graduating became a mining inspector.

In 1796 his mother passed away, leaving him with a substantial income. He left his job and started making plans for a scientific expedition. He chose Aimé Bonpland, a botanist, as his assistant. The two men traveled to Madrid, Spain and got special permission and passports from King Charles II to explore South America.

They spent the next five years traveling throughout South America and Mexico. While studying the flora and fauna of the Orinoco River basin in Venezuela, the two men mapped over 1,700 miles of the river, thus giving Humboldt the title of the father of geography. During their journey the two attempted to climb two mountains, one of which was Mt. Chimborazo, at the time believed to be the tallest mountain in the world. They were stopped from completing the climb up Mt. Chimborazo at an elevation of around 18,000 feet by a wall-like cliff.

Humboldt's explorations then took him into Mexico. While there, he worked with the Mexican Government on mining reform and gave lectures at the mining academy. He was offered a position in the Mexican cabinet but turned it down.

After a short stay in Cuba, he traveled to Washington D.C. in 1804, where he stayed for six weeks. President Jefferson was very interested in his work and invited Humboldt to spend three weeks with him. During this time Humboldt had several meetings with President Jefferson and the two became good friends.

At the age of 35, Alexander returned to Europe, ending a unique scientific journey. He settled in Paris for a short time, lecturing at the *Institute National*. When he realized that most of his fortune was gone, having spent the money on his travels and reserving the rest for publishing his findings, he returned to Berlin where he accepted a professorship. The king was so impressed with his work that he gave Alexander a stipend without any responsibilities attached to it. This was the first time Germany had done this. (The last time they did this was for Albert Einstein). With this new income, Humboldt again returned to Paris.

Alexander gave many lectures on his discoveries and wrote several books. His lectures were so well attended that new larger assembly halls had to be found. His first published work was a 33-volume collection called *The American Journey,* which detailed his work done in South America. Over half of the volumes detailed the plants and animals that he and Bonpland had observed. He is credited with being the first to really record the interactions between plants and climate and to recognize interactions between plants and animals. This is why he is often cited as the father of ecology.

The second major work was named *Kosmos,* which was an effort to fully describe the whole world from all scientific viewpoints. The last of the five volumes was published after his death.

Later in life, Von Humboldt was invited to Russia by the Tsar, where he explored much of that country. He recommended weather stations be set up around the country and using the data from these stations he determined that the interiors of continents have more extreme weather than along the coast. He also developed the first isotherm map—a map that has lines of equal average temperatures.

So, is Humboldt remembered in the United States? Well, there are eight townships named after him, one bay in California, and three states that have counties that bear his name—not bad for a man who only spent six weeks in the country.

GRASSLANDS

Swaying in the breeze

LESSON 8

What is a grassland?

Words to know:

grassland

semi-arid

prairie

pampa

savannah

steppe

When you think of zebras, lions, and hyenas what type of land do you picture in your mind? Do you think of a wide open area with tall grass blowing in the wind? This is a description of the African grassland called the savannah.

A **grassland** biome is an area where the main vegetation is grass. Grasslands usually have many different varieties of grass. Some grass grows only a few inches high; other grasses grow 2–3 feet high. And some grass, such as pampas grass, can be over 10 feet tall. Although grass is the dominant plant, grasses are not the only plants to be found in a grassland environment. Wildflowers including sunflowers, coneflowers, milkweed, and sage are plentiful and make the grassland very beautiful in the spring. There are usually only a few trees such as willows and cottonwoods that grow mostly near streams.

Grasslands receive 10–30 inches (25–50 cm) of rain per year. This is generally too dry for most trees to survive. Areas such as grasslands, that are wetter than deserts, but still fairly dry have a **semi-arid** climate. Grasslands usually have distinct wet and dry seasons. Because of this, the plants and animals that survive in grasslands are designed to survive prolonged periods of drought. Many plants go dormant and quit growing when water is scarce, but then begin to grow again when water becomes available. Others grow very long roots to reach water deep underground. Many animals can conserve water; others migrate to wetter areas and return when the rain returns. Grasslands generally have warm summers and cold winters.

Grasslands have periodic fires. Often when the grasses dry out, a lightning strike can start a grass fire. This may seem like it would destroy the ecosystem. Even though trees and shrubs are often killed by the fires, the main growing part of grass is below ground so the fire burns up the dry leaves, but does not kill the plants. This actually recycles the nutrients in the leaves, adding them back into the soil to be reused.

Grasslands have several different kinds of animals that survive well. Grazing animals are the ones most associated with grasslands. These are the animals that eat the grass. Zebras, antelope, deer, bison, wild horses, and gazelles are a just a few examples of grazing animals. Many different grazing animals can survive in the same area because different animals eat different parts of the grass plant. Some grazers eat just the tops of the grass. Other grazers prefer the middle section of the grass stems. Others will eat the lower portions of grass. This provides food for several different species from the same plant. And since the main growing area of the grass is below or near the ground, grass will grow back even if most of the top of the plant has been eaten.

Grasslands also have many burrowing animals that make their homes in the ground. These animals come out of their burrows to find food, but spend a significant amount of time underground. Burrowing animals that you might find in a grassland include prairie dogs, gophers, and jack rabbits. Burrowing often helps to break up the soil so that water can penetrate the ground and help the plants to grow better.

Finally, there are many carnivores that feed on the grazers and burrowing animals. Carnivores include eagles and hawks, coyotes, foxes, lions, snakes, hyenas, and jackals. Without these carnivores, the grazing animals would soon pass the carrying capacity and begin to die off.

Grasslands are called by many names throughout the world. In North America they are called **prairies**. In South America they are called the **pampas**. In Africa grasslands are called the **savannah**, and in Europe and Asia they are called the **steppe**. Although nearly every continent has large grasslands, the different species of plants and animals vary from region to region. The prairies are dominated by antelope and at one time they were filled with bison. There are many varieties of grass. The trees that grow near rivers in the prairie are usually cottonwood, oak, or willow. The savannah is home to elephants, lions, warthogs, and wildebeests. There are usually only one or two varieties of grass growing in a given area of the savannah. The trees found in the savannah are usually acacia and pine trees.

A black wild horse on the Russian steppe

GRASSLANDS WORKSHEET

Whenever you learn about a new biome you will be asked to complete a biome summary worksheet for your notebook. On this worksheet you will have to fill in information about the climate, locations, animals, and plants of that biome. The basic information needed to complete the worksheets will be included in the lessons. However, you can feel free to read more about each biome in other sources and include other information on your worksheet. In addition to the worksheet, you should try to include pictures of the plants and animals that are found in that ecosystem. You can look on the Internet, use clip art, take photos, or draw your own pictures.

Today, complete the "Grasslands" summary worksheet and add it to your notebook. Find pictures of plants and animals from various grasslands and add them to your notebook as well. Try to include plants and animals from prairies, savannahs, pampas, and steppes.

DIFFERENT VARIETIES OF GRASS

Purpose: To recognize the various types of grass available in your area

Materials: grasses growing in a natural area, flowering plants field guide, newspaper, heavy books, cardstock or heavy paper, page protectors

Procedure:

1. Visit a natural area where plants are allowed to grow wild. Collect samples of as many different kinds of grass as you can find. Try to include the leaves, flowers, and seeds if possible.

2. Use a field guide to help you identify the various types of grass that you collect.

3. When you return home, press the grass between sheets of newspaper by placing heavy books on top of the paper until the grass is dry.

4. Glue your samples to cardstock or other heavy paper. Label the types of grass and place in a clear page protector. Add your samples to your notebook.

5. If you like, you can include samples of non-wild grass such as the grass growing in your yard, as well as wheat, corn or other crop grasses.

The steppes have wild horses, and Saiga antelope. The grass that grows in the steppe is usually shorter than the grass that grows in the prairies. In the Pampas in South America you will find Pampas deer, Geoffroy's Cats, and rhea birds, which are related to ostriches. The famous Pampas grass is very tall and often used as ornamental grass in yards. Shorter grass also grows in the Pampas. Soil in grasslands is usually very fertile; this is why much of the grassland around the world has been turned into farmland or grazing land for domesticated animals.

God's design is evident in many aspects of the grasslands. From the ability of grasses to grow even after being eaten over and over to the design of different animals to eat different parts of the plant, we see God's hand in making the grassland a very efficient and beautiful place. ■

FUN FACT

Tropical grasses can grow as much as 1 inch (2.5 cm) per day.

WHAT DID WE LEARN?

- Name three characteristics of a grassland biome.
- What are four different types of grasslands?
- Where can each of these grasslands be found?

TAKING IT FURTHER

- Why are there few trees in a grassland?
- How do many plants survive extended periods of drought in the grassland?
- How can grass survive when it is continually being cut down by grazing animals?

GROWING GRASS

God designed grass plants to provide food for many of the world's animals. Grasses grow from the bottom of the plant, allowing the top to be eaten over and over again. God also designed the grazing animals with special digestive systems that can digest grass. A human could not survive on grass, but cattle, horses, antelopes, and other grazing animals have very special stomachs that can break down grass.

Humans have a single-chambered stomach. Food enters at one end, chemicals are added, and the food is moved around and broken down before leaving the other end of the stomach. However, grazing animals have three- or four-chambered stomachs. The food enters the first chamber where bacteria begin the digestive process. Many grazing animals then regurgitate their food and chew it more. When swallowed the second time, the food then enters the second chamber where digestive chemicals are added. The food continues on into the other chambers of the stomach where it continues to be broken down. Both the design of the grass and the design of the grass eaters demonstrate the genius of their Creator.

Purpose: To demonstrate grass's ability to regrow even when it is continually cut down

Materials: grass plants, scissors, ruler, "Growing Grass" worksheet

Procedure:

1. Obtain four similar grass plants. Place them together in a pot filled with potting soil.

2. Number four craft sticks from 1–4. Place one stick next to each plant.

3. Water the grass as needed to keep the soil moist, but not soggy.

4. Cut off the top ⅓ of plant 1. Cut off the top ⅔ of plant 2. Cut off almost all of plant 3—leaving only about ¼ of an inch of grass remaining above the soil. Do not cut anything off plant 4.

5. Measure the height of each plant and record your measurements in the appropriate column of day 1 on the "Growing Grass" worksheet.

6. Measure and record the height of each plant each day for the next three days (days 2–4).

7. After three days, again cut plants 1, 2, and 3 as you did in step 4.

8. Measure and record the height of each plant each day for three more days (days 5–7).

Questions:

- How did cutting the grass affect its ability to grow?

- Did one plant grow more than the others?

- How does this experiment demonstrate God's provision for grassland animals?

Conclusion:

You should find that cutting the grass does not negatively affect its ability to grow; cutting may actually encourage the plants to grow more.

FORESTS

Filled with trees

LESSON
9

Have you ever been in a forest? In a forest, you are surrounded by trees that tower over your head. It may be somewhat dark in the forest because the tall trees block out much of the sunlight. If you are quiet you can hear some of the many animals that make their home there.

An ecosystem that is dominated by trees is called a **forest**. There are several different kinds of forests depending on climate and latitude. Near the equator, where there is abundant rainfall and consistently warm temperatures, we find the tropical rainforests. As we move away from the equator we find deciduous forests that have broadleaf trees that lose their leaves in the winter. Finally, as you move farther north, you find the coniferous forests that are filled with evergreen trees such as pine and fir.

There are many differences between the various kinds of forests, and we will examine many of these differences in the following lessons. But there are also some similarities between the various forests, and we are going to learn about some of the similarities in this lesson. Because many trees grow closely together in a forest, the plants in a forest tend to grow in distinct layers. The top layer is called the **emergent layer**. This is where you find the tops of the tallest trees. These trees rise above the other trees

WHERE WOULD I LIVE?

Complete the "Where Would I Live?" worksheet and identify the layer of the forest in which you are most likely to find each animal.

Grasslands & Forests

and look like they are poking out of the roof of the forest.

Most of the mature trees form the next layer down, which is called the **canopy**. This is the roof of the forest. Because the trees of a forest usually grow close together, their branches and leaves often block out most of the sunlight, making it relatively dark inside the forest.

The third layer down is the **understory**. This layer consists of two different groups of trees. Some of the trees in the understory are young trees that will continue to grow and eventually become part of the canopy. Other trees in the understory are different species, which may be shorter and are designed (or have adapted) to grow with less sunlight.

Below the understory layer is the **shrub layer**. Here you will find shorter plants including many varieties of shrubs. Again, the shrubs that grow in a forest must be able to survive and thrive with less sunlight than other shrubs that grow in more open areas.

Below the shrub layer is the **herb layer**. This is where you will find small plants such as grass, flowers, ferns, and seedlings. Finally, the lowest layer of the forest is the called the **floor**. The plants that live on the floor include lichens, mosses, and fungi. This layer is also called the litter layer because you will find fallen trees and branches, as well as leaves and other decaying material here.

FUN FACT

Forests cover 1/3 of all land in the world and contain 2/3 of the leaf surface area of all land plants.

There are many animals that live in forest biomes. And just as the plants grow in distinct layers, most animals spend the majority of their lives in only one or two layers of the forest. Birds may swoop down to the forest floor to catch their prey, but they generally take it back to their nests to eat it; thus they spend most of their time in the canopy or emergent layers. Similarly, monkeys that live in the canopy may occasionally leave the trees, but quickly return, spending most of their lives in the canopy. Other animals spend their entire lives on the forest floor. Therefore, you must study each layer of the forest to fully understand the whole ecosystem. ■

WHAT DID WE LEARN?

- What are the major plants in a forest?
- What are the six layers of a forest?
- Which layer forms the roof of the forest?
- Name three kinds of forests.

TAKING IT FURTHER

- Why is the forest floor relatively dark?
- Why is it important to study each layer of a forest?
- How might new trees find room to grow in a mature forest?

TREE ANATOMY

Trees are truly amazing creations of God. They begin as tiny seeds but can grow into giants of the forest. To appreciate how this happens, we need to understand the anatomy of a tree. So let's take a look inside a tree trunk to understand how a tree grows, how it transports all of the water and nutrients, and how it stays strong enough to support all of its branches and leaves.

On the outside of a tree is its outer bark. The outer bark protects the tree from insects, fire, and other hazards. If we could peel back the bark and look inside the tree trunk we would find that just inside the bark is the phloem or inner bark. This part of the tree carries food that is produced in the leaves to the rest of the tree. These cells have a relatively short life and eventually die and become part of the outer bark.

Just inside the inner bark is a layer of cells called the cambium. Cambium cells are constantly growing and dividing to produce new cells. The new cells toward the outside of the tree become new phloem cells. The new cambium cells toward the inside of the tree become new wood cells. The continuous production of new cambium cells in the spring and summer causes the bark and wood to become thicker and stronger as the tree gets older.

The cambium produces larger light colored cells in the spring and smaller dark colored cells during the summer. This causes the inside of a tree trunk to have rings. The relative size of the rings indicates the growing conditions for the year. Smaller narrow rings might indicate a period of dry weather, whereas wide rings likely indicate very favorable growing conditions.

As we move inward from the cambium, we find the sapwood or xylem. The sapwood is the part of the tree that carries the water and nutrients upward from the roots to the rest of the tree. These are the vital ingredients that the leaves need for performing photosynthesis. Just like the phloem cells, the xylem cells only live a short time and eventually die. When they die, they become part of the inner wood of the tree called the heartwood. Although heartwood is no longer living and transporting materials, it provides the needed strength for the tree to support the weight of all the branches and leaves.

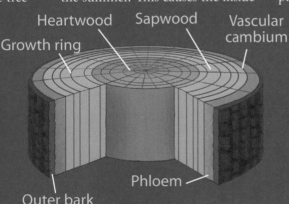

Heartwood Sapwood Vascular cambium
Growth ring
Outer bark Phloem

Activity:

Draw a diagram of the layers of a tree trunk showing the bark, phloem, cambium, sapwood, and heartwood. Add this diagram to the forest section of your notebook.

TEMPERATE FORESTS

Can you see the forest for the trees?

LESSON 10

What is a temperate forest?

Words to know:

deciduous forest

deciduous tree

coniferous forest

coniferous tree

evergreen tree

boreal forest

taiga

Temperate forests are located in the temperate zone between the tropics and the polar regions. They receive more rain than grasslands but less rain than a tropical rainforest. There are two main kinds of temperate forests: deciduous forests and coniferous forests.

Deciduous forests contain many kinds of plants, but the most abundant plants are deciduous trees. **Deciduous trees** are trees with broad leaves that shed their leaves each autumn and grow new leaves in the spring. Deciduous forests can be found in Japan, eastern China, western Europe, Asia, eastern Australia, and eastern North America.

Deciduous forests grow in areas that receive from 30–60 inches (75–150 cm) of rain each year. These areas of the world experience four distinct seasons. The temperature in the deciduous forests varies greatly depending on the time of year. Winters are cold and summers are generally warm and wet. Wintertime temperatures can be as low as -20°F (-30°C) and summer temperatures can be as high as 85°F (30°C), but the average yearly temperature in a deciduous forest is around 50°F (10°C).

Common trees found in deciduous forests include oak, maple, beech, and elm trees. Common shrubs include rhododendron and huckleberry. You will also find a variety of wildflowers such as bluebells and primroses. The forest floor also has many mosses, ferns, and fungi.

The animals that live in a deciduous forest are as diverse as the plants that grow there. You will find many birds from bald eagles to grouse. You will also find opossums, black bears, white-tailed deer, squirrels, and rabbits. In Australia you will also find the duck-billed platypus.

Because the winters are often cold and trees lose their leaves, the food supply in the winter is much less than it is in the summer. Therefore, God has equipped many animals to survive the harsh winter conditions by hibernating, or going into a deep sleep during the winter, thus using less energy and needing less food. Other animals migrate to warmer areas in the winter and return in the spring or summer. So the animals you see in the summer are often different from those you see in the winter.

Because the trees lose their leaves in the fall, deciduous forests are extremely beautiful in the autumn. The leaves of different trees turn a variety of colors as the trees quit producing chlorophyll in preparation for winter. So before the leaves fall, a forest can become a sea of various shades of red, yellow, and orange. Eventually, the leaves dry up and fall off, leaving bare branches to weather the cold winter.

Another type of temperate forest is the coniferous forest. **Coniferous forests** are dominated by **coniferous trees** that bear seeds in cones instead of having flowers and fruit, as most deciduous trees do. Coniferous trees are **evergreen trees**—they do not lose their leaves in the fall. Other names for specific coniferous forest regions in the north include the **boreal forest** and the **taiga**.

Coniferous forests also experience warm summers and cold winters. The winters tend to be colder than in deciduous forests, and the amount of precipitation is less as well. Coniferous forests receive 12–33 inches (30–80 cm) of precipitation each year, much of which comes in the form of snow.

FUN FACT

The largest coniferous trees, the giant redwoods and sequoias, grow in the forests of northern California. These trees contain more biomass than any other living plant. Some of these giant trees are nearly 3,000 years old.

TREE IDENTIFICATION

One of the first things you need to know about a forest is what kind of trees are growing there. You can learn to identify trees by comparing their leaves with the pictures in a tree guide. When you do this you must first ask yourself some questions:

1. Are the leaves broad and flat or are they needle-like?

2. If they are broad, are the edges smooth, toothed, or lobed?

3. If they are broad, do the leaves grow across from each other, or alternating along the twig?

4. If they are needle-like do they grow singly or in groups?

5. If they grow in groups how many needles are in a group?

6. How long are the needles?

These questions will help you find where to look in the field guide to find the type of tree you are looking for.

If you have the opportunity, take a tree guide to a forest and use it to identify the trees that you find growing there. If you do not have a nearby forest, you can practice identifying trees by their leaves by completing the "Tree Identification" worksheet.

FOREST WORKSHEETS

Complete the "Deciduous Forest" and "Coniferous Forest" summary worksheets and add them to your notebook. Find pictures of plants and animals from various forests and add them to your notebook as well. Be sure to include pictures showing the autumn colors of the deciduous forest.

FUN FACT

The cones of some evergreen trees, such as the lodgepole pine, do not open to release their seeds unless they experience the heat of a forest fire. This prevents the trees from becoming too crowded, but ensures that the forest will be reseeded in the case of a fire.

Because of these harsher conditions, the main trees in coniferous forests are evergreen trees that have needle-like leaves instead of broad, flat leaves. Common trees found in coniferous forests include spruce, fir, and pine trees. Although evergreen trees are the most common kinds of trees, there are often deciduous trees such as aspens mixed in with them. Other plants in a coniferous forest include poison ivy, columbines, ferns, and mosses. Lichens also flourish in the coniferous forest biome.

Coniferous forests are the largest type of land biome, covering approximately 17% of the land. They cover about 50 million acres (20 million hectares) of land. Coniferous forests can be found in North America, Europe, and much of Asia, as well as in many mountain regions around the world.

In spite of the harsh conditions in the winter, the coniferous forest is home to many different kinds of animals. You will find foxes, wolves, Dall sheep, bighorn sheep, caribou, lynx, badgers, owls, and beavers. Many of these animals sleep or hibernate in the winter to conserve energy, just as many of the animals in a deciduous forest do.

Coniferous forests are often dotted with lakes. Many of these lakes were carved out by glaciers that covered much of the northern latitudes during the Ice Age. These lakes and their accompanying streams provide water for the abundant wildlife found in these forests. ■

WHAT DID WE LEARN?

- What are some characteristics of a deciduous forest?
- What are some characteristics of a coniferous forest?
- What is another name for a coniferous forest in the far north?
- What is a deciduous tree?
- What is a coniferous tree?

TAKING IT FURTHER

- What are some ways that plants in temperate forests were designed to withstand the cold winters?
- What are some ways that animals in temperate forests were designed to withstand the cold winters?
- Would you expect plant material that falls to the floor of the coniferous forest to decay quickly or slowly? Why?

FOREST JEOPARDY

Complete the "Forest Jeopardy" worksheet by writing questions for the answers that are given on the worksheet.

TROPICAL RAINFORESTS

Growing where it's wet

LESSON 11

What is a rainforest?

Words to know:

tropical rainforest

arboreal

Forests that grow where there is abundant rainfall, at least 80 inches (200 cm) per year, are called **tropical rainforests**. Tropical rainforests grow near the equator, between the Tropic of Capricorn and the Tropic of Cancer. They are found in Central and South America, Africa, India, Southeast Asia, and western Australia.

Because of the abundant rainfall, rainforests are very humid and have many rivers flowing through them. Because they are near the equator, the temperature in rainforests does not change much. The temperature in a rainforest is usually between 70 and 85°F (20–30°C).

Many plants and animals thrive in this warm, humid environment. Just a few of the animals include spider monkeys, gibbons, tree frogs, lizards, lemurs, boa constrictors, anacondas, bats, capybaras, ibis, piranhas, and toucans. In fact, more than half of the land animals and birds in the world live in the tropical rainforest. Many of the animals are **arboreal**, which means that they live in the trees and seldom come down to the ground. And although there are many different kinds of animals, mammals are more rare in the rainforest than in other biomes. Birds, on the other hand, are more abundant.

The rainforest is also home to many different kinds of plants. One study in a six-acre area of a rainforest found 141 different species of trees. Many tropical plants have become important agricultural products. Some plants you might recognize

FUN FACT

Since the rainforest receives so much rain, many of the nutrients in the soil are washed away. The soil is actually more fertile in the grasslands than it is in the rainforests.

RAINFOREST WORKSHEET

Complete the "Tropical Rainforest" summary worksheet and add it to your notebook. Find pictures of plants and animals from the rainforest to include as well.

RESEARCHING RAINFOREST ANIMALS

Purpose: To better understand the animals that live in the rainforest

Materials: research materials

Procedure:

Choose one animal that lives in the tropical rainforest and write a report on it to include in your notebook. Include pictures of your animal as well. Be sure to find the answers to the following questions:

1. What does it eat?

2. Which layer(s) of the forest does it live in?

3. What are its predators?

4. What unusual or interesting habits does it have?

5. What interactions does it have with other animals?

(but not realize that they were originally found in tropical forests) include pineapples, oranges, bananas, lemons, eggplant, peppers, and cocoa. Today, most of these plants are grown on plantations in tropical areas, but wild plants can still be found in the rainforests.

Another important rainforest plant is chicle, which is used to make chewing gum. Latex, which is used in making many products including rubber and paint, comes from rubber trees that grow in the tropical rainforest. Also, balsa and mahogany trees, which are prized for their wood, are tropical forest trees.

The plants in the rainforests are also very important for producing medicines. About one-fourth of all medications are made from plants that grow in the tropical rainforests. The main ingredient in aspirin comes from the rainforest as well as the plants used to make many antibiotics. Quinine, the medication used to treat malaria, also comes from a tropical rainforest plant.

Because the trees in the forest block most of the sunlight from reaching the forest floor, there are not many plants growing on the floor.

The largest Banyan tree in North America is in Fort Myers, Florida.

FUN FACT

Although we often associate the word jungle with the rainforest, a jungle is technically an ecotone, an area between the tropical rainforest and a tropical grassland. There are fewer trees in a jungle which allows for more plant growth near the ground.

Instead, some plants grow on the sides of the trees where there is more sunlight. These plants are called epiphytes. Epiphytes are plants that use other plants without taking nutrients from them. There are many different epiphytes in the rainforest. Seventy percent of all orchids are epiphytes. Some ferns and cacti are also epiphytes.

One very unusual epiphyte is the banyan tree. The seeds of the banyan are dispersed by birds that eat the fruit of the banyan. When a seed lands on a branch of a tree it may germinate and a new tree begins to grow. The seedling sends out roots that grow down the side of the host tree. As the banyan grows larger, it sends out prop roots which grow out of the bottom of its own branches. Eventually, the roots of the banyan trees may completely enclose the host tree. Thus the banyan is sometimes called a strangling fig tree. Banyan trees can continue to spread out as they put out more and more prop roots from their branches. One banyan tree was measured covering ¾ acre of land. Banyans are very long-lived trees; some are more than 300 years old. ■

FUN FACT

The long vines that Tarzan swings from are called lianas.

WHAT DID WE LEARN?

- List some ways in which a tropical rainforest is different from a temperate forest.
- Where are the rainforests located?
- What is an arboreal animal?
- What is an epiphyte?
- Name at least one epiphyte.

TAKING IT FURTHER

- Do you think that dead materials would decay slowly or quickly on the floor of the rainforest? Why?
- If you transplanted trees such as orange, cacao, or papaya trees to a deciduous forest, would you expect them to survive? Why or why not?
- Which animals are you most likely to see if you are taking a walk through the tropical rainforest?

RAINFOREST PRODUCTS

You are an advertising executive. Your job is to promote products from the rainforest. Choose one or more products discussed in the lesson or choose from the list below. Then design an advertising campaign to encourage people to use products from the tropical rainforest. Include your advertising materials in your notebook.

Items from the rainforest:

1. Coffee
2. Brazil nuts
3. Cashews
4. Allspice
5. Cinnamon
6. Cloves
7. Ginger
8. Black pepper
9. Avocado
10. Papaya
11. Guava

UNIT 3

AQUATIC ECOSYSTEMS

THE OCEAN

Marine ecosystem

LESSON 12

What lives in the ocean?

Words to know:

phytoplankton

sunlit zone

euphotic zone

zooplankton

twilight zone

disphotic zone

midnight zone

aphotic zone

benthos

nekton

plankton

Challenge words:

bioluminescent

Three quarters of the surface of the world is covered with water, so it should not surprise you that many of the world's ecosystems occur in or near the water. The ocean contains 95% of all surface water and is the world's largest ecosystem. Although we generally divide the ocean into five different oceans (Pacific, Atlantic, Indian, Arctic, and Antarctic), the oceans are really all connected together and form one ocean.

The ocean is perhaps the most important ecosystem in the world. The ocean greatly affects the weather around the world. It also drives the water cycle by providing the large surface from which most evaporation occurs. It contains fish and other animals that feed a large portion of the people in the world and it provides a multitude of jobs for people. Therefore, it is very important to understand the ocean ecosystem.

Because of its vast size, it is difficult to define a single ocean ecosystem. Different areas of the ocean have different conditions and thus have different habitats. However, there are many characteristics that are the same around the world and we will examine some of these characteristics in this lesson.

As you learned earlier, virtually all ecosystems depend on the producers, the organisms that produce food by photosynthesis. In the ocean most of the photosynthesis takes place in microscopic creatures called **phytoplankton**. These creatures are algae and other small organisms that contain chlorophyll and produce food for other creatures in the ocean.

FUN FACT

More than half of all photosynthesis in the world occurs in the ocean by the phytoplankton that live there.

OCEAN WORKSHEET

Complete the "Ocean" summary worksheet and add it to your notebook. Find pictures of marine algae, plants, and animals to include as well.

CURRENTS DISTRIBUTE NUTRIENTS

Currents are very important to life in the ocean. Not only do currents move the plankton from place to place, but the currents also move oxygen and nutrients. This helps to keep the ocean an active, living place.

Purpose: To see how currents distribute nutrients in the ocean

Materials: shallow pan, water, food coloring

Procedure:

1. Fill a shallow pan with water and place it on a level surface.

2. Gently blow across the surface of the water. Notice how your breath moves the water, making small waves and currents.

3. Drop a few drops of food coloring at one edge of the water.

4. Again, gently blow across the surface of the water. Watch how the food coloring is distributed throughout the water.

Conclusion:

This is an indication of how currents transport nutrients, oxygen, and plankton around the world.

Aquatic Ecosystems

Since photosynthesis requires sunlight, the life in the ocean changes as you go deeper because the sunlight can only penetrate a limited depth. The upper layer of the ocean is called the **sunlit zone** or **euphotic zone** and consists of the top 660 feet (200 m) of water. This is where you will find most living creatures and nearly all of the plants and phytoplankton. You will find endless varieties of fish, jellyfish, sharks, coral, shrimp, lobsters, and most other sea creatures. You will also find **zooplankton**—microscopic organisms that eat the phytoplankton and then become the food of many other animals in the ocean.

FUN FACT

The average depth of the ocean is 12,451 feet or nearly 2 ½ miles. This is five times the average height of land formations. Although the ocean is relatively shallow near the shore, it is very deep in other areas.

As you go deeper, the sunlight decreases. At depths from 660 to 3,300 feet (200–1,000 m) there is limited sunlight. This part of the ocean is referred to as the **twilight zone** or **disphotic zone**. There are no plants or phytoplankton here because there is not enough light for photosynthesis. The animals that live in the twilight zone must be able to survive in very low light, be able to live in cold water, and be able to stand great pressure on their bodies. You will find octopi, a few fish, such as the coelacanths and viper fish, and a few crabs and eels.

Below 3,300 feet (1,000 m) there is no sunlight even in the daytime. This part of the ocean is called the **midnight zone** or the **aphotic zone**. Only a few animals live in this dark, cold, high pressure environment. Most of the animals that live in the disphotic and aphotic zones are scavengers that eat dead and decaying material that filters down from above, or predators that eat the other animals. Some animals move vertically through the layers, while others spend most of their time in only one layer.

The living organisms in the ocean can be divided into three groups. The **benthos** are the plants and animals that live on the ocean floor. In areas that are relatively near the shore, the water is all in the euphotic zone, so many plants and algae attach themselves to the ocean floor. These organisms that live on the ocean floor are considered bottom dwellers. Clams, crabs, worms, and other burrowing animals are part of the benthos as well as starfish, snails, and sponges.

The second group of organisms is the **nekton**. These are animals that are free moving. Fish, whales, shrimp, lobsters, squid and many other sea creatures can swim where they like. Their movement does not depend on the currents of the ocean.

Finally, **plankton** are algae (phytoplankton) and animals (zooplankton) that drift with the ocean currents. They live near the surface and cannot overcome ocean currents by swimming. These are the organisms that form the bottom of most food chains in aquatic environments.

All of the plants and animals that live in the ocean must be able to live in a saltwater environment. The ocean is about 3% salt. All together, there are 55 different elements that have been identified in seawater. In 1,000 grams of water there are about 35 grams of minerals. Of the minerals in the seawater, about 75% is salt, although the salt concentration varies from place to place.

In addition to minerals, gases such as oxygen, nitrogen, and carbon dioxide are also dissolved in the water. The concentration of oxygen is highest near the surface of the ocean. Some oxygen dissolves from the air into the water, but most of it is produced by phytoplankton, primarily algae, that grow near the surface of the water.

As you study the ocean, you will gain a greater appreciation for the amazing ecosystems that God has set up around the world. ■

The huge whale shark feeds on plankton.

Aquatic Ecosystems

WHAT DID WE LEARN?

- How much of the earth is covered with water?
- How much of the surface water of the world is in the ocean?
- How many oceans are there?
- What are the three zones that the ocean can be divided into?
- What are the three major groups of living organisms in the ocean?

TAKING IT FURTHER

- What might happen in the ocean if the currents stopped flowing?
- Why do most animals in the ocean live in the euphotic zone?
- Why might the aphotic zone occur at a shallower depth than 660 feet (200 m) in some areas?

UNDERSTANDING BIOLUMINESCENCE

Although most sea creatures live in the sunlit zone, some of the most interesting creatures in the ocean live in the twilight and midnight zones. Many of these creatures can make their own light, which is handy in an environment with little or no light. Animals which can produce their own light are said to be **bioluminescent**. Research bioluminescent animals and make a report to include in your notebook.

Many jellyfish are bioluminescent.

Activity

Draw a population pyramid for an aquatic food chain. Be sure to start with algae or some other phytoplankton. See if you can make it at least four levels high. Include this drawing in your notebook.

Coral Reefs

Underwater wonderlands

LESSON

13

What is coral?

Words to know:

coral reef

atoll

fringing reef

barrier reef

Challenge words:

coral bleaching

One of the most beautiful ecosystems within the ocean itself is the coral reef. A **coral reef** is a limestone formation built from the exoskeletons of millions of tiny invertebrates called corals. Coral reefs are found in warm, clear water near the equator, in the tropical zone. Reefs are almost always found in water that is less than 150 feet (45 m) deep.

Coral polyps are creatures that build the foundation of the coral reef. An individual coral polyp is a tiny tube-like creature with tentacles. It resembles an upside down jellyfish. The polyp builds a protective exoskeleton around itself and spends much of its time inside its protective shell.

Corals use their tentacles to sting and pull in tiny prey, but corals receive most of their energy from a special type of algae that lives inside of them and performs photosynthesis, thus providing food for both the algae and the corals. Corals must live in clear waters in order for the sunlight to reach the algae. If the water becomes murky, the algae cannot perform photosynthesis and the corals can die.

There are over 400 different species of coral. Most corals are named for the shape of the colonies that they build. Corals of the same species will live very closely together. As they grow, their exoskeletons merge together to form colonies. Some colonies look like fans; others look like horns or even brains. As corals die, new coral polyps will build their homes on top of the dead exoskeletons, thus increasing the size of the reef.

In addition to the corals, there are thousands of other animal species that make their homes in the coral reef. Sponges, shrimp, sea stars, and moray eels are just a few of the wide variety of marine animals you might find. There are also over 1,500 species of fish that have been found living near coral reefs. This includes clown fish and butterfly fish. You will also find green turtles, sea

CORAL REEF WORKSHEET

Complete the "Coral Reef" summary worksheet and add it to your notebook. Find pictures of plants and animals from the coral reef to include as well.

CORAL MODEL

Coral colonies grow in a wide variety of shapes. Examine pictures of several different types of coral, then use modeling clay to build your own coral colony. Be sure to take a picture of your model and include it in your notebook.

anemones, sea urchins, octopi, squid, and clams in a coral reef. A coral reef is a stunning array of shapes and colors because of the wide variety of life there.

Coral reefs generally grow in one of three different configurations. An **atoll** is a circular shaped coral reef that has formed around a sinking inactive volcano. An atoll usually encloses a shallow lagoon. A **fringing reef** is a reef that is attached to the mainland and grows out into the open water. A third configuration is a barrier reef. A **barrier reef** forms out in the ocean away from the shore. The reef forms a barrier that helps block waves from reaching the shore, thus giving it the name of barrier reef.

FUN FACT

There are more different species of organisms in the coral reef than in any other ecosystem except the rainforest.

The largest coral reef is the Great Barrier Reef off the northeast coast of Australia (shown at left). The Great Barrier Reef is the largest biological structure on earth and is even visible from the moon. It is 1,250 miles (2,000 km) long. The Great Barrier Reef is important in many ways. Not only is it beautiful and home to millions of animals, it protects the coastline of Australia from erosion by blocking much of the wave action. It is also a vital part of the commercial and recreational fishing industries in Australia.

Coral reefs grow fastest in areas with stronger wave action. Corals need calcium and other minerals in order to produce their exoskeletons. Waves bring new nutrients, enabling the corals to grow. Anyone who has ever visited a coral reef can attest to the wonder and beauty that God has created there. ■

Australia's Great Barrier Reef extends for 1,250 miles (2,000 km) along the northeastern coast of Australia.

WHAT DID WE LEARN?

- Where will you find coral reefs?
- What is a coral reef made from?
- Where do corals get most of their energy?
- What are the three main types of coral reefs?
- What are some of the animals that live in a coral reef besides corals?

TAKING IT FURTHER

- Why are coral reefs found in water that is usually less than 150 feet (45 m) deep?
- Why do corals grow best in swift water?

CORAL BLEACHING

The beautiful colors found in the coral reefs are due in large part to the algae living inside the corals. When two living organisms live together in a mutually beneficial relationship it is called symbiosis or mutualism. The corals provide protection for the algae and the algae provide food for the corals. This symbiotic relationship is vital to coral survival.

In the past 40 years many coral reefs have experienced a phenomenon called coral bleaching. Many of the corals have expelled their algae. This causes the corals to lose their main source of food. It also causes the corals to become white or clear in color, thus the name *coral bleaching* because color is removed.

Many times a coral that expels its algae will get new algae and become healthy again. In fact, some scientists believe that coral bleaching may actually be a protective mechanism that allows the coral to get rid of algae that are not suited to the environmental conditions and to gain new algae that are better able to survive.

Other times corals die because they cannot replace the algae and thus they do not get enough nutrients to survive. Many areas of coral around the world have died due to coral bleaching.

No one knows exactly what causes coral bleaching to occur. It is believed that the expulsion of the algae is a reaction to unusual stresses placed on the coral. Scientists have proposed several possible causes. Some people believe it occurs when the water temperature rises too much. Much of the coral bleaching that occurred on a wide basis in the 1980s and 1990s coincided with large El Niño years which may have affected the water temperature around the coral reefs.

A second possible cause for coral bleaching is an increase in ultraviolet radiation. If water is too still, too much ultraviolet radiation can reach the corals and damage the tissues. This is believed to be the cause of some coral bleaching. On the other hand, if water becomes murky it blocks out some of the sunlight. This causes the algae to perform less photosynthesis, which could also result in coral bleaching.

Another possible cause is disease. It may be that a virus or other pathogen is responsible for the way the coral reacts to the algae. Some scientists think that increased acid levels or other pollutants in the water could be responsible for some coral bleaching as well.

Today, scientists do not fully understand the mechanisms or triggers of algae expulsion. More testing and research are needed before we will truly understand the causes of coral bleaching. We know that God has designed many animals to be resilient and able to handle changes to their environment, and the future will show if coral bleaching is detrimental in the long term or just a way to better handle changing conditions.

Aquatic Ecosystems

BEACHES

Take a walk on the sand

LESSON 14

What kinds of beaches are there?

Words to know:

beach

dynamic equilibrium

inter-tidal zone

tide pool

Challenge words:

dune system

primary dune

secondary dune

maritime forest

Where the waters of the ocean meet the land, a shore is born. This shore is often called a **beach**. A beach is an actively changing ecosystem. The water is constantly bringing and depositing new materials. At the same time, the movement of the water is constantly wearing away the land along the shore. Most beaches are in a state of **dynamic equilibrium**. This means that the amount of material being deposited is approximately equal to the amount of material that is being eroded away.

The area of land along a beach that is covered by high tide and uncovered at low tide is called the **inter-tidal zone**. Plants, algae, and animals that live in the inter-tidal zone must be able to deal with constantly changing conditions. They spend part of the day partially or totally submerged in seawater and part of the day exposed to the sun and air. Many of these animals burrow into the sand or dirt to stay moist. Others have shells that protect them. These organisms are designed to conserve water.

The types of plants and animals that live along a beach depend greatly on the material that the beach is made of. Beaches are either rocky or sandy. Rocky beaches provide soil, cracks, and crevices that give plants a place to become firmly attached. These plants provide food and protection for many animals that would not live on a sandy beach. Along a rocky beach you are likely to find starfish, mussels, barnacles, and oysters. You will also observe sea lettuce, swamp periwinkle, and enteromorpha, which is a green algae that many people call seaweed.

Rocky beaches are best known for their **tide pools**. These are areas along the beach that fill with water when the tide is high, and remain filled after the tide goes out. The water in these tide pools is refreshed twice a day with the rising of

BEACH WORKSHEET

Complete the "Beach" summary worksheet and add it to your notebook. Find pictures of plants, algae, and animals from both rocky and sandy beaches to include as well.

MAKING SAND

Sand is an accumulation of sediment. Sand in different parts of the world is comprised of different materials. Some sand is mostly crushed coral. Other sand contains bits of rocks and broken seashells. Other sand is made of volcanic glass—rock that shattered when hot lava was suddenly cooled as it hit cold seawater. This is how the black sand beaches of Hawaii were formed. Much of the white sand around the world is made of quartz.

Purpose: To appreciate the forces required to make new sand

Materials: rocks, seashells, plastic zipper bag, safety goggles, towel, hammer, sand, magnifying glass

Procedure:

1. Place a few small rocks and/or seashells in a plastic zipper bag and close the bag.

2. Wrap the bag in a towel.

3. While wearing safety goggles, use a hammer to break the rocks and shells into small pieces.

4. Carefully remove the smallest pieces of debris from the bag. Compare your sample with a sample of sand. How are they similar? How are they different?

5. Use a magnifying glass to closely examine a sample of sand. Can you see the different shapes and colors of the grains of sand? If you have sand from more than one location you can see how different areas contain different kinds of sand.

Conclusion:

Although you may think of all sand as being the same, when you compare sand from various parts of the world, you will see that there are significant differences.

the tides. These pools provide a refuge from the winds and sun that dry out the rest of the beach.

Some of the plants and animals that you find on rocky beaches are also found on sandy beaches including gulls and other shore birds, but because the shifting sand does not provide a solid foundation, there are also different plants and animals on a sandy beach. You are more likely to find sand dollars, crabs, shrimp, and clams on a sandy beach than on a rocky beach. Other animals you are likely to find at a sandy beach include horseshoe crabs and turtles. And although you will still find sea lettuce, you are not likely to find enteromorpha or periwinkle. ■

Ghost crab on the beach

WHAT DID WE LEARN?

- What is a beach?
- What are the two main kinds of beaches?
- What is the name of the area of land that is covered at high tide and uncovered at low tide?
- What are some animals you are likely to see in a beach ecosystem?

TAKING IT FURTHER

- Why might you find different plants and animals on a rocky beach from those on a sandy beach?
- How is new sand formed?
- Explain how a beach can be in dynamic equilibrium.

A DUNE SYSTEM

When you visit a sandy beach you can observe ecological succession in progress. Recall that succession is the process where one ecosystem is changing into another ecosystem. At a beach, as you move from the edge of the water toward the land, you can see one ecosystem change into another. This area is called a dune system.

The area of land closest to the beach is called the primary dune. Primary dunes develop where beach grass begins to grow. This grass anchors the dune by trapping sand and keeping it from eroding away. The grass has an extensive root system that pulls water from the ground and stabilizes the dune. The primary dune area has too much salt, wind, and sun for trees to grow, but the beach grass that grows here is tolerant to salt and can thrive even with varying amounts of salt. The grass provides nesting areas for many shore birds.

As you move inland from the primary dune the landscape changes from one of primarily grass to one of grass and shrubs. This area is called the secondary dune. In the secondary dune area you will find bayberry, scrub pine, yarrow, beach grass, and poison ivy. This more diverse plant life provides homes for more diverse animal life as well. Many small animals live in the secondary dunes.

Moving farther inland, you begin to see more trees. The area of shrubs and trees is called a maritime forest. This is not your usual forest. The trees in a maritime forest generally are short with twisted limbs. The limbs from these trees provide the interesting drift wood that many people like to collect.

If you have a chance to visit a beach, observe the changing ecosystem as you move inland from the shore. If you cannot visit a beach, look at pictures of beaches. Then draw your own picture of a dune system and include it in your notebook.

Aquatic Ecosystems

ESTUARIES

Where fresh and salty meet

What is an estuary?

Words to know:

estuary

salt marsh

salt meadow

mangrove forest

Challenge words:

watershed

One of the most productive ecosystems in the world is an estuary. An **estuary** is where freshwater flows into saltwater. The estuary is a productive ecosystem because the constant flow of freshwater into the ocean, coupled with the ebb and flow of the tides, stirs up nutrients that can be used by the many plants and algae that grow in the area. This stimulates plant growth, which in turn stimulates animal populations.

Although food is readily available, plants and animals in the estuary must deal with some difficult conditions as well. The salt level in the water is constantly changing. In the summer when there is relatively little rain and higher evaporation, the salt level in the estuary is considerably higher than in the winter when water does not evaporate as quickly and more freshwater is added by rain. Organisms must also deal with strong currents from the constantly changing water flow. This water flow also stirs up mud which can decrease the amount of oxygen available, so plants and animals must be able to cope with these conditions.

There are actually several different kinds of estuary ecosystems depending on which plants are most dominant. A **salt marsh** is an estuary in which rushes are the predominant plants. Farther inland, where the ground is somewhat drier, salt-tolerant grasses and small herbs and shrubs help create **salt meadows**. And in many areas mangrove trees are the dominant plant, making the estuary a **mangrove forest**.

Mangroves and other estuary plants are very important because they help to filter salt out of the water and help to filter silt and other materials so they do not enter the ocean. This is especially important in areas near coral reefs. The water must remain clear for the coral to thrive, and mangrove trees help to keep the water clear.

MIXING FRESH & SALTWATER

Saltwater and freshwater come together, sometimes forcefully, in an estuary. Saltwater and freshwater do not easily mix. The salt in the ocean makes the saltwater denser than freshwater so the freshwater tends to sit on top of the saltwater and slowly mix with it. You can conduct an experiment to see the effect that salt has on how water mixes.

Purpose: To compare the densities of freshwater and saltwater

Materials: four clear cups, water, salt, green and blue food coloring, eye dropper, marker

Procedure:

1. Fill four clear cups half full of water.

2. Use a marker to label two of the cups "Fresh" and two of the cups "Salty."

3. Add 2 teaspoons of salt to each cup that is marked "Salty." Stir to help the salt dissolve.

4. Add several drops of green food coloring to one cup of salty water. Stir the water. Add several drops of blue food coloring to one cup of freshwater and stir the water.

5. Use an eyedropper to add several drops of green saltwater to the clear cup of freshwater. What happened to the green water? It should sink to the bottom of the cup.

6. Use an eyedropper to add several drops of blue freshwater to the cup of clear saltwater. What happened to the blue water? It should float on top of the saltwater.

7. Allow the cups to sit for several minutes. What happened to the colored water? Eventually the freshwater and saltwater will mix, but it may take several hours.

Conclusion:

Saltwater and freshwater have different densities so they do not readily mix. This causes the density and saltiness of the waters in estuaries to vary. Plants and animals that live in the estuaries are able to deal with changing salt levels

Aquatic Ecosystems

There are over 50 different species of mangrove plants worldwide.

In addition to the many plants that live in the estuary, there is a wide variety of animals. There are many mud snails and marine worms that thrive on the mud that is stirred up by the moving water. These animals eat the mud and help to recycle the nutrients. Cockles and other shellfish filter food out of the water. The water in the estuary is full of many varieties of fish including mullet, flounder, and sole. The areas near the water are home to a wide variety of birds such as the bittern, rail, heron, tern, stork, and pelican. Sea lions and other marine animals also live in or near some estuaries.

Some animals in the estuary are seasonal. Many of them migrate to other areas and return during certain times of the year. Some animals, like birds, fly to other parts of the world. Other animals, such as the freshwater eel, swim upstream and later return to the estuary. Some animals swim farther out to sea during certain seasons and later return to the estuary. So the animals you observe at one time of the year could be very different from those you see at a later time. ■

ESTUARY WORKSHEET

Complete the "Estuary" summary worksheet and add it to your notebook. Find pictures of plants and animals from the various types of estuaries including mangrove forests, salt marshes, and salt meadows.

WHAT DID WE LEARN?

- What is an estuary?
- Name three types of estuaries.
- What are some plants you might find in an estuary?
- Name several animals that you might find in an estuary.

TAKING IT FURTHER

- Why is an estuary a very productive ecosystem?
- How do mangrove trees help coral reefs?
- Why is the salt level in the water constantly changing in an estuary?
- Why might you find different estuary animals in the same location at different times of the year?

WATERSHEDS

Things that happen on land can have a huge effect on water ecosystems because the water that flows across a farmer's field or even in your yard eventually flows into a river and finally flows into the ocean. All of the land that has water flowing into a particular river or body of water is called a watershed.

Your yard is part of several watersheds. When you water your grass whatever water is not used by the grass flows into the ground and eventually finds its way to an underground river. So your yard is part of the watershed for that underground river. The underground river will eventually reach ground and flow into a river above ground. Your yard will be a

Mississippi River Delta

part of the watershed for this above ground river as well. Finally, that river may flow into the ocean, making your yard part of the watershed for the ocean, too.

One of the most important watersheds in the United States is the Mississippi River Basin. 41% of the continental United States eventually drains into the Mississippi River, making it the largest watershed in the United States and the third largest watershed in the world. Most of the land from the Rocky Mountains to the Appalachian Mountains is part of this watershed.

The Mississippi River starts at Lake Itasca in Minnesota and flows over 2,300 miles to the Gulf of Mexico. As it flows southward, several major rivers join it including the Missouri, the Ohio, the Arkansas, and the Tennessee Rivers. When the Mississippi River reaches the Gulf of Mexico its freshwater flows out into the salty gulf. The water does not immediately mix with the water in the gulf. In fact, NASA satellites have shown that the freshwater flows through the gulf, around the tip of Florida, and into the Gulf Stream of the Atlantic Ocean before it becomes thoroughly mixed with the saltwater.

Where the Mississippi River flows into the Gulf of Mexico is called the Mississippi River Delta. This is one of the most important estuaries in the world. The River Delta contains approximately 3 million acres (12,000 km²) of coastal wetlands and 40% of the salt marshes in the continental United States.

You can find out about the watershed near your home by visiting the "Surf Your Watershed" website from the US Environmental Protection Agency. http://cfpub.epa.gov/surf/locate/index.cfm.

Aquatic Ecosystems

Lakes & Ponds

It's fresh

LESSON 16

What is the difference between a lake and a pond?

Words to know:

lake

pond

overturn

algae bloom

Lakes and ponds are some of the most beautiful ecosystems in the world. Crystal clear water filled with fish, ducks, and other water birds can inspire and turn your heart to God. Many lakes were carved out by the movement of glaciers during the Ice Age. Other lakes fill the craters of extinct volcanoes.

Lakes are large bodies of freshwater. Although lakes are filled with freshwater instead of saltwater, a deep lake has many of the same characteristics as the ocean. A deep lake has a euphotic or sunlit zone and an aphotic or midnight zone just like the ocean. And the plant and animal life found in each zone is different. Also like in the ocean, the main source of food at the bottom of the food chain is photosynthetic algae. Large lakes can also have beaches like the ocean, but without the distinct tides of the ocean. **Ponds** are lakes that are shallow and do not have an aphotic zone.

Lakes and ponds can be found all around the world. And although the specific organisms vary somewhat, there are many similar organisms found in lakes around the world. Algae, water lilies, and some grasses grow in the water. Along the edge of lakes you are likely to find grasses, rushes, cattails, sedges, sagebrush, and thistles.

The animals that live in lakes and ponds include zooplankton such as rotifers and tiny crustaceans as well as many kinds of frogs, toads, turtles, and insects. However, fish are probably the animals most closely associated with lakes. Trout, perch, walleye, bass, and sturgeon are only a few species of fish that are found in lakes around the world.

LAKES & PONDS WORKSHEET

Complete the "Lakes and Ponds" summary worksheet and add it to your notebook. Find pictures of plants and animals that live in or near lakes and ponds to include as well.

FREEZING FRESH & SALTWATER

Purpose: To observe how freshwater and saltwater freeze

Materials: two clear cups, water, salt, thermometer, marker, "Watching Water Freeze" worksheet

Procedure:

1. Fill two clear cups ¾ full of water.

2. Label one cup as "Freshwater" and the other cup as "Saltwater."

3. Add 2 teaspoons of salt to the "Saltwater" cup and stir to dissolve.

4. Measure the temperature of the water in each cup and record the temperatures on the "Watching Water Freeze" worksheet.

5. Place both cups in a freezer.

6. Measure the temperature of the water in each cup every 10 minutes for 60 minutes. Record your measurements and observations on the worksheet.

Conclusion:

As freshwater freezes it expands so ice will form on the surface of the water first. You will not see ice forming on the bottom of the cup. This is a demonstration of God's provision for life in the lakes and ponds.

The salt in the saltwater helps to keep the water molecules apart, making it hard for the water to freeze. It should take much longer for saltwater to begin to freeze, and if your freezer is close to 32°F (0°C) it may not freeze at all. This is an example of God's provision for life in the oceans as well.

Other animals live near lakes and depend on the lake for water. Birds such as cranes, pelicans, egrets, ibis, swans, ducks, and geese are common on or near lakes. Beaver, deer, and moose are also commonly found near lakes.

Since algae is the main source of food for the animals that live in a lake, it is important to understand how God provides the needed nutrients for these tiny organisms to survive. The density of freshwater changes as it cools. As water cools it becomes denser until it reaches 37°F (4°C) at which point is expands as it freezes and becomes less dense. This causes ice to float on the surface of the lake. In the spring, as the ice begins to melt, the cold water on the top of the lake is more dense than the warmer water deeper down. When enough ice has melted, this dense, cold water rapidly sinks to the bottom of the lake. This causes the warmer water to rise, stirring up the mud on the bottom of the lake. This action is called **overturn**. Overturn is important because it releases oxygen and many of the nutrients that have become trapped on the bottom of the lake, thus providing nutrients for the algae and other plankton.

Overturns in the spring have been known to cause **algae blooms**, a sudden growth in algae that can turn the surface of a lake or pond green. After a few days or weeks, the algae growth slows down and the other animals that eat the algae enjoy abundant food. A similar overturn usually occurs in the fall as the top layer of water begins to cool. However, this does not usually result in an algae bloom.

The changing density of water is a gift of a loving Creator who designed the water to preserve life in the lakes and ponds. Not only do overturns release nutrients for algae growth, but the fact that ice floats is truly amazing. No other common substance becomes less dense when it freezes. But because frozen water is less dense than liquid water, it floats. This provides an insulating barrier during the winter for the animals that live in the lakes and ponds. If ice did not float, lakes and ponds would freeze solid and the animals would die. ■

Ice fishing is possible because lakes freeze at the top, allowing the fish to survive underneath.

WHAT DID WE LEARN?

- What is a lake?
- What is a pond?
- What are two ways that lakes were formed in the past?
- What is an overturn?
- What is an algae bloom?

TAKING IT FURTHER

- Why is overturn important to lake ecosystems?
- Why does an algae bloom often occur in a lake in the spring?
- In which lake zone would you expect to find most small creatures like rotifers?
- What would happen to fish during the winter if ice did not float?

THE GREAT LAKES

One of the most amazing areas in the world is the Great Lakes region of the northern United States and southern Canada. These lakes hold more than 18% of the world's surface freshwater. The lakes cover 95,000 square miles (246,000 km²) and their watershed covers 288,000 square miles (746,000 km²). The Great Lakes have over 9,000 miles (14,500 km) of shoreline.

These amazing lakes are not only important for the habitat they provide for the fish and other aquatic animals that live there, but there are approximately 35 million people that depend on this ecosystem for water and for their livelihood. Recreation on the lakes is a $15 billion per year industry. Sport fishing is a $4 billion per year industry. In addition, the lakes provide a major traffic route for shipping.

The fish in the Great Lakes have always been abundant. The lakes contain trout, perch, walleye, whitefish, and salmon. The lakes also provide habitat for a wide variety of birds including the bittern, goshawk, meadowlark, and many species of waterfowl.

Because people as well as animals depend on these lakes, constant vigilance is needed to meet the needs of both groups. When people build dams and other structures that stop or slow down the flow of water into the lakes, it has an effect on the plants and animals in that ecosystem. For example, building dams on the rivers flowing into the lake makes it difficult for salmon to return to their birthplaces in the rivers for spawning. This has caused the salmon population to decrease in the Great Lakes. Many groups have been formed to help oversee development around the Great Lakes to ensure that people and animals can both enjoy this beautiful ecosystem.

Human interaction is not the only problem facing the Great Lakes. Many species of animals have been introduced that were not native to the area. Some of these animals do not have natural predators in the area and are crowding out the native species. Some invasive species include sea lampreys, zebra mussels, and rusty crayfish. People are trying to find ways to control the populations of these species and to protect native populations.

There is so much to learn about the Great Lakes that you should do some research on your own. Then take what you have learned and make a Great Lakes page for your notebook. In addition, make a map of the Great Lakes to include in your notebook and complete the "Great Lakes Fact Sheet," too. There is room on the fact sheet to add some facts of your own as well.

FUN FACT

The Great Lakes are so large that they create their own weather systems. One weather phenomenon caused by these large bodies of water is called *lake effect snow*, which brings snow to many nearby cities including Chicago.

Satellite image of the Great Lakes

RIVERS & STREAMS

Flowing water

LESSON 17

Why can't the same animals that live in lakes live in rivers?

Words to know:

river

stream

riparian zone

tributary

Do you enjoy the gentle trickle of a small stream or the majesty of a great waterfall? Then you enjoy the beauty of a river ecosystem. **Rivers** and **streams** are ecosystems that contain flowing freshwater. Although many of the same animals that live in lakes also live in rivers and streams, the current of the river makes it difficult for some plants and animals to survive here. The current also allows more oxygen to become dissolved in the water, allowing different species to thrive.

Although lakes and the ocean get most of their food from the photosynthesis performed by algae, there is very little algae in most rivers and streams. Much of the energy in the river ecosystem comes from the breaking down of leaves and other plant materials that fall into the water. The trees and other plants that grow along the banks of a river contribute to the food supply of the river.

Just as with lakes, in a river there are many animals that live in the water, and many other animals that live on the banks or regularly visit the river. Some of the animals that live in rivers include snails, salamanders, and many varieties of fish including trout and salmon. Other animals that live near and depend on the water include snakes, herons, eagles, insects, turtles, raccoons, muskrats, storks, ducks, otters, deer, and bears.

Although there are few plants in the water, some algae can survive in the moving waters. There is abundant plant life along the banks in what is called the **riparian zone**. These plants include grasses, pussy willows, willow trees, alders, elkslip, and water hyacinths. The plants in the riparian zone provide habitat for the many animals in the area.

RIVERS & STREAMS WORKSHEET

Complete the "Rivers and Streams" summary worksheet and add it to your notebook. Find pictures of plants and animals that live in or around rivers to include in your notebook.

Aquatic Ecosystems

Riparian plants also help to filter the river runoff.

Moving water can be a powerful force. As the water flows downhill it picks up bits of rock, sand, silt, and other debris. The faster the water is flowing, the more debris (and larger debris) it can carry. As a river reaches a flat area it slows down and begins to drop the sediment it was carrying. Slow-moving rivers tend to flow in lazy curves. As the water goes around a curve it deposits more sediment on the inside of the curve because the water is flowing more slowly there and picks up sediment on the outside of the curve, since the water is flowing more quickly there. This causes the curves to get bigger over time. The plants and animals that thrive in and near fast moving water are often different from those that thrive near slow moving water.

Large rivers seldom start out large at their source. Water flows downhill because of gravity. When rain falls at higher elevations, the water flows into small streams. Streams flow and eventually join together to form small rivers and then small rivers flow into larger rivers. A smaller stream or river that flows into a larger river is called a **tributary**. Some rivers have only a few tributaries, but most rivers have many tributaries. ■

FUN FACT

The Nile River is the longest river in the world. The Missouri/Mississippi River is the longest river in the United States. The Amazon River has the largest river basin in the world and thus drains water from more land than any other river.

RIVERS OF THE WORLD

On a copy of the "Rivers of the World" worksheet, draw in and label the major rivers of the world on the world map. Below is a list of rivers to include.

- Amazon
- Congo
- Nile
- Mississippi

- Yangtze
- Rio De La Plata
- Hwang Ho/Yellow River
- Orinoco

- Yukon
- Volga

WHAT DID WE LEARN?

- What is a river?
- Where does most of the energy for a river ecosystem come from?
- Name some plants you might find in a river ecosystem.
- What is a tributary?
- What is the riparian zone?

TAKING IT FURTHER

- Why do fewer plants grow in the water of a river than in a lake or ocean?
- Would you expect a river to be larger at a higher elevation or a lower elevation?
- Do rivers move faster over steep ground or in relatively flat areas?
- Would you expect water to cause more erosion in a steep area or in a relatively flat area?

RIVER FACTS

There are so many interesting rivers in the world that it is worth doing a little investigation and learning more about some of the major rivers. Learn what you can about each of the rivers listed in the activity above, complete the "Rivers Fact Sheet," and include it in your notebook.

Aquatic Ecosystems

The Amazon River

Biggest river in the world

Dark jungles, fierce warriors, and some of the deadliest animals on earth; these are some of the images many of us have of the Amazon River—the biggest river in the world. But what do we really know about the Amazon?

The first record of this river's exploration was by a Spanish adventurer named Francisco de Orellana, in 1541. Orellana told of being chased by fierce women warriors during his exploration, so the king of Spain named the river the Amazon after the mythological female Amazon warriors.

For centuries people have known that the Amazon is the biggest river in the world, but its true length has only recently been measured. Using the most modern measuring techniques, some people now claim that the Amazon may also be the longest river. Its length is very close to that of the Nile. The Amazon is approximately 4,000 miles (6,400 km) in length while the Nile is approximately 4,160 miles (6,695 km), only a little longer. Measuring the length of a river is not an exact science so different studies sometimes come up with slightly different numbers.

The Amazon supplies 20% of the freshwater going into the ocean. That is more water than the next top 10 rivers of the world combined! The flow rate of the Amazon is 10 times greater than that of the Mississippi River. The river is so large it moves 106 million cubic feet of suspended sediments into the ocean each day. That would be equal to about 1 million pickup trucks full of dirt and debris dumping their loads into the ocean each day. The Amazon's flow at its mouth is 53 million gallons per second (200,000 m³/sec). The Nile's flow is only around 925,000 gallons per second (3,500 m³/sec), or less than 2% of the Amazon's flow.

The Amazon is so large that an ocean liner can sail about half way up it, or 2,000 miles inland. It's one of the few large rivers that is not crossed by a bridge. This makes it easier for boats to navigate the river, but hinders land traffic.

During the dry season the river is considerably smaller than during the rainy season. During the dry season the width of the Amazon River varies between 1 and 6 miles, but when the rains begin to fall, the river swells to over 30 miles wide. Not only does its width increase but it becomes much deeper, too. Its depth may rise by as much as 50 feet in many areas during the rainy season. The water floods the forest, keeping many of the trees partially to mostly submerged for five months out of the year.

The Amazon River Basin is the largest watershed in the world. Water flows into the river from an area about the size of the continental United States. The Amazon drains nearly half of Brazil, as well as land in Peru, Ecuador, Bolivia, and Venezuela. There are over 1,000 tributaries that drain into the Amazon.

So what else makes the Amazon unique? Like all rivers, the Amazon has its own ecosystem, but because of its size, the Amazon River ecosystem is different from any other river ecosystem in the world. The Amazon is sometimes called the River Sea because of its vast size. So you might expect to see some similarities between the Amazon River ecosystem and an ocean ecosystem, and you do. Many of the animals that you find in the ocean have freshwater equivalents in the Amazon River, and the interactions between these animals are similar to what you find in parts of the ocean.

One of the most famous animals that lives in the Amazon River is the piranha. But did you know that there are 20 different species of piranhas in the Amazon? Unlike the image of a ferocious attacker, many piranhas eat plant material. Others do eat meat, mostly fish, and only the red-bellied piranhas swarm in larger schools or packs and can speedily strip flesh off of an animal.

The Amazon River is also home to freshwater dolphins. The Amazon River dolphin, or boto dolphin, is considered the most intelligent of the freshwater dolphins. It has the ability to turn its head from side to side as it swims, which aids greatly when hunting for fish to eat. Boto dolphins use echolocation, or sound waves similar to sonar, to hunt. This ability also gives them the ability to swim through the submerged trees during flood season, which is where many of the fish live during this time.

The tucuxi dolphin looks similar to a bottlenose dolphin found in the ocean. However, it is much smaller than either the bottlenose dolphin or the boto dolphin. The adult tucuxi dolphins are around 110 lbs. (50 kg), whereas the boto can be up to 440 lbs. (200 kg).

Dolphins are not the only large animals in the river. The large size of the Amazon River allows some fish to grow without the restrictions of smaller rivers and lakes. Catfish weighing over 200 lbs. (90 kg) have been captured. Also, the largest freshwater fish in the river is the arapaima. These fish can weigh as much as 440 lbs. and be as long as 15 feet (4.5 m). They are one of the most popular food fish in South America.

Large animals also live on the surface of the water. The Amazon River is home to the anaconda snake, sometimes called the water boa. It lives in water and swamps in and near the Amazon. The female green anaconda can grow up to 32 feet (10 m) long and weigh up to 550 lbs. (250 kg), but averages around 20 feet (6m) long. They can eat fish and small mammals but can also eat crocodiles and deer, swallowing them whole.

There are thousands of small animals that live in and around the Amazon River, too. There are over 1,000 types of frogs that live there. Turtles also live in the water and lay their eggs on the banks of the river during the dry season, providing food for many of the animals that live along the river's shore, in addition to producing more turtles.

The Amazon is unique in both its size and diversity with many more interesting animals than we could possibly cover here. So if you are interested, you can do more research by getting books from your local library or searching the Internet.

UNIT **4**

EXTREME ECOSYSTEMS

TUNDRA

Is it frozen?

What is tundra?

Words to know:

tundra

Arctic tundra

Antarctic tundra

Alpine tundra

ephemeral

permafrost

Challenge words:

papillae

The northernmost lands of Canada, Alaska, Scandinavia, Greenland, and Russia are often considered a frozen wasteland. These northern areas are very cold and covered with ice and snow much of the year. But don't let the forbidding appearance fool you. There are many plants and animals that survive in this cold land.

Areas that are treeless, with long cold winters and cool summers are called **tundra**. Tundra comes from the Finnish word *tunturi*, which means treeless plain. Most tundra is located above the Arctic Circle and is often called **Arctic tundra**. A small amount of **Antarctic tundra** exists on Antarctica, and tundra conditions exist near the tops of many mountains and are called **Alpine tundra**.

In the Arctic tundra, the winters are very long. In the winter there are many weeks with little or no sunlight and the temperatures can be very cold with average temperatures as low as -30°F (-34°C). However, the summers are very different. The average temperatures are 37–54°F (3–12°C). The sun stays in the sky for many weeks without setting.

Extreme Ecosystems

FUN FACT

In Point Barrow, Alaska, the most northern point in the United States, the sun rises around May 11 and does not set again until around August 1, providing 83 days of continuous sunlight. On the other hand, the sun sets around November 18 and does not rise again until around January 23, resulting in about 65 days of continual darkness.

Alpine tundra

This provides a growing season of 50–60 days.

Although most plants cannot survive in these harsh conditions, God has designed many plants that can survive. Many of these plants are considered **ephemerals**, which are plants with an accelerated life cycle. Many of these plants can go through their complete life cycle from germination to fruit and seed production in less than two months. There are over 400 varieties of flowers as well as sedges, rushes, cinquefoil, heather, and a few small shrubs that live in the Arctic tundra. Also mosses and lichens flourish in the tundra.

Not only do most plants have an accelerated life cycle, but they are specially designed for the tundra in other ways as well. Most plants in the tundra are small and low to the ground. This helps them to withstand the high winds that are common in the winter. Many of the plants have a fuzzy appearance. These small hairs help to protect the plant from wind and help to insulate the plants as well. Plants generally grow together in clumps, providing further protection from wind and cold.

The tundra does not receive much precipitation, usually only 6–10 inches (15–25 cm) per year, mostly in the form of snow. This does not mean that the tundra is filled with dry land. The land in the tundra is actually filled with ponds and bogs in the summertime. This happens because the soil does not defrost more than a few inches on the surface. This perpetually frozen layer is called **permafrost**. The permafrost stops melting ice and snow from draining, so the surface of the land actually stays very wet during the summer, providing the needed moisture for plant growth.

Various animals also live in the Arctic tundra. Many of these are large mammals such as polar bears, caribou or reindeer, and moose. Smaller animals also abound including Arctic foxes, lemmings, Arctic ground squirrels, and swarms of mosquitoes. The tundra swan, Canada goose, and rock ptarmigan are a few of the birds you will find in the tundra, especially in the summer months. The Antarctic tundra is home to many types of penguins.

Like the plants, many of the animals in the tundra also have an accelerated life cycle. For example, the northern robin feeds its young 21 hours a day and the baby birds mature in only eight days.

FUN FACT

The Arctic tundra has the lowest species count on earth.

TUNDRA WORKSHEET

Complete the "Tundra" summary worksheet and add it to your notebook. Find pictures of plants and animals that live in the tundra to include in your notebook.

Southern robins require 13 days to mature. God has equipped these animals to survive the short summers.

God has also equipped animals on the tundra to survive the long cold winters. Many animals hibernate during the winter in dens that are insulated from the extreme cold. Other animals migrate to warmer climates in the winter and only return to the tundra in the summer. Although the tundra is a difficult ecosystem for most plants and animals, it is far from barren. It supports a wide variety of plant and animal life. ■

ANIMALS CHANGING COLORS

Many animals in the tundra change color to match the environment. Some are brown or grey in the summer and turn white as winter approaches and the land becomes covered with snow. The Arctic fox, Arctic hare, and ptarmigan are all animals that are white in the wintertime. This provides them with camouflage from their predators. Baby seals are also white, providing them a measure of protection while on land. Polar bears, who spend most of their lives on ice floes, are white all the time.

Purpose: To appreciate how white fur or feathers provide protection to tundra animals

Materials: small box, white cotton balls, white tissue paper or white quilt batting, photos of Arctic animals with white fur or feathers

Procedure:

1. Fill a small box with white material to represent snow. You can use cotton balls, strips of tissue paper, pieces of quilt batting, or other white materials.

2. Place photos of Arctic animals with white fur or feathers such as foxes, polar bears, baby seals, and ptarmigans among the white material in the box.

3. Step back a few feet and see how well the animals blend in with their surroundings. Their coloring helps to protect them from their predators.

TWO LAYERS OF FUR

Many mammals in the tundra have two layers of fur. The first layer is very short and close to the body. This provides a layer of insulation to help trap heat next to the skin. The second layer is longer and provides a second layer of insulation to further trap heat and to keep out chilling wind. In the summer, many of these animals lose their longer fur since it is not needed during the warmer days. They then grow a new coat of fur as winter approaches.

Purpose: To appreciate how two layers of fur help to keep an animal warm

Materials: large bowl of ice, two pairs of gloves (one pair must fit inside the other, for example one could be cotton gardening gloves and the other could be leather work gloves)

Procedure:

1. Fill a large bowl with ice cubes.

2. Place a thin glove on one hand and then place a larger thicker glove over the thin glove on the same hand. You now have one hand that is uncovered while the other hand is covered with two layers of protection.

3. Hold both hands over the ice. Can you feel the cold from the ice with each hand?

4. Push both hands into the ice for a few seconds. How cold do each of your hands feel?

Conclusion:

You should find that two layers of protection keep your hand quite comfortable, while no protection leaves your hand very cold. God's design of two layers of fur, helps many animals survive the cold winters in the tundra.

POLAR BEARS

When you think of ice and snow you probably think of polar bears. These cuddly-looking giants have captured the hearts of many people. However, these bears are not cuddly pets; they are the largest predators on land. An adult male weighs 660–1300 pounds (300–600 kg) and a female weighs about half as much as a male.

Polar bears spend a large part of the time hunting for their favorite food, which is the ringed seal. They will dive from the sea ice into the frigid waters to catch their prey or they will wait by a seal's air hole until it surfaces and then attack. Polar bears swim from one piece of ice to another to follow the movement of the seals. Polar bears have an extremely good sense of smell and can detect a seal more than a mile away. Although polar bears prefer seals, they eat many other animals as well. They eat fish, beluga whales, and have even been known to eat caribou.

Polar bears are specially designed for swimming as well as for travel across the frozen ice of the tundra. Their bodies are streamlined for efficient swimming. Also, they have a thick layer of blubber which makes them more buoyant in the water and helps to insulate them from the cold temperatures. Their toes are somewhat webbed, helping them to be very good swimmers. Polar bears can swim for more than 60 miles (97 km) at a time.

On land the polar bear's large paws help to spread out its weight so it can more easily move across the snow. Also, its soft pads are covered with tiny papillae or small bumps, which help to give the bear traction on the ice.

Although a polar bear looks white, its fur is actually translucent. Light reflects off of the hollow hair shaft, making it appear white. As a polar bear ages it may appear more yellow or even greenish. This happens when algae begins to grow inside the hair shafts. Its fur is oily and does not mat so the bear can easily shake off the water after it emerges from the sea.

A female will have her first babies when she is around 4 or 5 years old. She will go on land and dig a snow cave. There she will give birth to one or two tiny babies. A baby polar bear weighs only about 1 pound (2.5 kg) at birth, but it grows very quickly. At the end of winter the mother and her cubs emerge from their winter den. Babies nurse for about 2 to 2½ years.

In 2008 polar bears were declared a threatened species by the United States government. Although they are protected from hunting by all countries in which they live, there is some concern that global warming may be reducing the sea ice on which the bears hunt. The extent of global warming and the long term effects are not agreed on by all scientists. More research is needed to determine the effect on polar bears.

Extreme Ecosystems

ROBERT E. PEARY

1856–1920

In search of a land without an east or west

Has there ever been anything you've wanted to do your whole life? Is it something dangerous that no one has ever done before, like being the first person to make it to the North Pole? That was the dream of a young boy by the name of Robert Peary—a dream he made come true.

Robert was born on May 6, 1865 in Cresson, Pennsylvania. When Robert was two years old, both of his parents became sick; his mother recovered but his father did not. After the death of his father, Robert and his mother moved to Maine. There, Robert spent much of his time hiking in the woods and exploring new areas. He preferred the solitude of the woods to being around people. This time spent in the woods enabled him to become self-reliant, which was an important aspect of his character.

After high school, Robert went on to earn his civil engineering degree and later joined the U.S. Navy. Before leaving for his first assignment, Robert met an African-American store clerk by the name of Matthew Henson, in Washington D.C. After talking with Henson, Robert learned that they shared the same passion for exploration. Henson joined the Navy expedition, and the two become lifelong partners and friends. Matthew Henson was with Peary on every expedition he went on from that point.

Lt. Peary's first assignment was to Nicaragua where he worked on the Inter-oceanic Ship Canal Project, whose goal was to explore the possibility of putting a canal across Nicaragua. In 1886 Peary and Henson went on their first expedition to the interior of Greenland. Here, Peary and Henson learned about dog sledding, hunting, fur clothing, and building an ice shelter from the Inuit people. These skills would prove invaluable in the future.

In 1888 Robert Peary married Josephine Diebitch and the couple, along with Henson, made two trips to McCormick Bay, half way between the Arctic Circle and the North Pole. After these two trips Josephine stayed home while Peary and Henson made several more trips to Greenland during the 1890s. There they spent much of their time exploring. During this time Robert Peary discovered that Greenland was an island and he also discovered three very large iron meteorites in Cape York.

After discovering that Greenland was an island, Peary decided the best place to launch an expedition to the North Pole was Ellesmere Island. From there he made several attempts to reach the North Pole with his final and successful attempt starting in 1908. He left New York with a group of 23 men on the *Roosevelt* and sailed to Ellesmere Island, Canada. The party wintered there as they prepared for the trip and conditioned themselves to the cold.

On March 1, 1909 they set off for the North Pole. Over the next month several small groups, which had been with them to help move supplies, turned back and returned to the base camp. This was done in order to set up points along the way where supplies would be stored for Peary's return trip. On April 7, 1909 Robert Peary, Matthew Henson, and four Inuits reached what they and the world thought was the North Pole. It has been learned in recent years that his calculations were off slightly because of the shifting ice and he may have been off by 30 to 60 miles. Nevertheless, the world hailed Peary as a hero and he is credited with the first successful trip to the North Pole.

Two years later Admiral Peary retired from the Navy and took up writing. He produced three books about his explorations. The hard life of the north had prematurely turned Peary into an old man, and he passed away in 1920 at the age of 63. He is buried at Arlington National Cemetery.

His lifelong friend Matthew Henson was mostly ignored by the public until 1937 when he was admitted as a member of the Explorers Club in New York. Henson died in 1955 at the age of 89. In 1988 Henson's remains were moved from New York to a site close to Robert and Josephine Peary in Arlington National Cemetery. In 1945 Congress awarded Henson a silver medal for outstanding service to the U.S. Government. And in 2000 the National Geographic Society awarded the Hubbard Medal to Henson posthumously for distinction in exploration, discovery, and research—identical to the one awarded to Peary in 1906.

DESERTS

Sand and more sand

LESSON 19

What different kinds of deserts are there?

Words to know:

desert

cold desert

hot desert

succulent

stomata

transpiration

dromedary camel

Bactrian camel

nocturnal

estivate

mirage

When you think of a desert, do you picture waves of heat rising from a sea of sand? That is what most people think of as a desert. And many deserts are very hot, dry, and sandy. But some deserts can be very cool. A **desert** is a biome that receives less than 10 inches (25 cm) of rain per year. Most deserts receive less than 6 inches (15 cm) of rain per year.

Deserts are generally divided into two groups: hot deserts and cold deserts. **Cold deserts** are dry areas where the daytime temperature drops below freezing during part of the year. The Atacama Desert in Chile, the Gobi Desert in China and Mongolia, and the Great Basin of the western United States are all cold deserts.

Hot deserts are dry areas that do not experience freezing temperatures. The average temperature in a hot desert is 68–77°F (20–25°C), but don't let these numbers fool you. Hot deserts can be very hot during the day in the summertime, often reaching temperatures of 109–120°F (43–49°C). Because deserts are so dry, the temperature drops very quickly when the sun sets; so even though the daytime temperature may be very hot, the desert can become very cool at night. Hot deserts can be found around the world. Some of the largest hot deserts include the Arabian Desert which covers most of the Middle East, the Mojave Desert of the southwestern United States, the Sahara Desert in Africa, and the Australian Desert in Australia.

> **FUN FACT**
>
> The hottest temperature ever recorded in the Sahara Desert was 136°F (58°C).

Saguaro cactus

Extreme Ecosystems

Deserts often lose more moisture to evaporation than they gain from precipitation. Thus, the environment is very dry. You might expect that there would be very little life in the desert. Although it is true that many plants and animals cannot survive in such a harsh environment, there are actually many plants and animals that are specially designed to live in the desert. Both plants and animals that live in the desert can conserve water, storing it for use during the long dry periods.

Many plants that live in the desert are **succulents**. These plants have fleshy stems that can absorb and store large amounts of water when it rains so it will be available to the plant later. Many types of cacti and aloe vera plants are examples of desert succulents. Other plants you are likely to find in the desert include the sagebrush, mesquite, Joshua tree, creosote bush, and desert trumpet.

When green plants perform photosynthesis, they usually suck up more water from the ground than they use and release that water into the air through tiny holes in their leaves called **stomata**. This process is called **transpiration**. But desert plants cannot afford to release excess water into the air. So God has designed them to conserve water. Succulents often have needles instead of leaves. These needles help prevent the plant from losing water through transpiration, thus conserving the water that is stored. Other plants have leaves but the leaves have very few stomata. This design also helps to conserve water.

Despite harsh conditions, many animals live in the desert. You are likely to see the spadefoot toad, lizards, kangaroo rats, voles, badgers, scorpions, burrowing owls, ostriches, roadrunners, and vultures. There are also many desert snakes including rattlesnakes, coral snakes, and sidewinders. In many deserts you may also find camels. Camels with one hump are called **dromedary camels** and are native to hot deserts in Africa and the Middle East. Two-humped camels are called **Bactrian camels** and are native to the Gobi Desert. Because the Gobi is a cold desert, the Bactrian camels grow a coat of long hair over their short hair for the winter and shed the long hair in the summer.

Like plants, the animals that live in the desert have many ways to cope with the dry climate and extreme temperatures. First, most animals are **nocturnal**, meaning they

FUN FACT

The saguaro cactus, the one most often associated with deserts, only grows in the Sonoran desert in Arizona, California, and Mexico. The saguaro can grow up to 50 feet tall, weigh several tons, and live for 200 years.

DESERT WORKSHEET

Complete the "Desert" summary worksheet and add it to your notebook. Find pictures of plants and animals that live in the desert to include in your notebook.

STORING WATER

Purpose: To demonstrate how plants can conserve water

Materials: thin plastic bag, such as a produce bag

Procedure:

1. Fold a plastic bag accordion style along the length of the bag with each fold about 1 inch wide.

2. Notice the diameter of the bag. This represents a cactus when it has been dry for a long period of time.

3. Carefully fill the bag with air, holding the air in the bag with your hand. Notice what happens to the size of the bag as it fills up. The diameter expands. This is what happens to the stems of cacti as they fill with water.

4. Slowly release the air from the bag. Gently refold the creases to return the bag to its original size. This is what happens to the stems as the plants use up the water.

Conclusion:

The stems of many desert plants are folded like the bag was in this experiment. When water is available, the plant fills up and the folds are pushed out, making room for a large amount of water. When water is not available, the water in the plant is used up and the stems shrink back down.

sleep during the hot day and are active at night when the temperatures are more bearable. Also, many animals can conserve water. Camels can store large amounts of water. Other animals **estivate**, which means they go into a deep sleep during the summer when it is hottest and awake in the fall or winter when temperatures cool down.

Not only do deserts receive only a small amount of precipitation, the water they do receive does not come in regular intervals. Deserts often go months or even years between rainstorms. When it does rain, there are often flash floods. The ground has become very dry and hard and water does not easily penetrate it. Thus when a large amount of rain falls all at once, it often rushes through canyons and much of it does not sink into the ground.

Rain brings a dramatic change to the desert. Where there was mostly dry brown foliage, the rain produces a rainbow of colors from all of the blooming plants. When water is available, the plants and animals get to work. Just as in the tundra where the growing season is short, many of the plants in the desert are also ephemerals—plants with accelerated life cycles. Many desert animals also have accelerated life cycles. The spadefoot toad can grow from egg to tadpole in only nine days!

In between the rains, the desert dries out. Much of the water evaporates instead of soaking into the soil. As the water evaporates it leaves behind any minerals that were dissolved in it. Salt is the most common mineral that is dissolved

The desert tortoise estivates in summer.

in water, and when water evaporates the salt is left behind. Many deserts have large salt flats where salt has been deposited for hundreds of years.

As the ground dries out, wind often whips the sand and soil around, slowly building massive dunes in some deserts. A dune can be started as prevailing winds blow sand against a clump of plants creating a small hill. The wind carries sand uphill until gravity pulls it back down. This creates a smooth slope on the windward side and steep slope on the other side of the plants. If wind continues to blow in the same direction, a dune will slowly form.

In addition to building and moving dunes, wind can cause problems for living things in the desert. The wind can pick up massive amounts of sand or dirt, creating giant dust clouds and sand storms. The sand can bury plants and cover the homes of animals. The sand also wears away rocks and other structures in its path. People and animals have learned to seek shelter from the desert storms.

The heat in the desert can cause an interesting phenomenon. As the sun heats the earth, the air near the ground becomes hot and rises. This hot air can bend the light from the sun, resulting in a reflection of the sky onto the ground. This makes it look like there is water on the ground where there really is no water at all. This phenomenon is called a **mirage**. Thirsty travelers have been known to be tricked by mirages.

Even though the desert is a harsh environment, the plants and animals that live there are diverse and beautiful. We cannot forget that even in the desert evidence of God's design is everywhere. ■

A mirage in the Sahara Desert

WHAT DID WE LEARN?

- What is a desert ecosystem?
- How is a cold desert different from a hot desert?
- What are some plants you would expect to find in the desert?
- What are some animals you would expect to find in the desert?
- What is the difference between a Bactrian camel and a Dromedary camel?

TAKING IT FURTHER

- In what ways are plants well suited for the desert environment?
- In what ways are animals well suited for the desert environment?
- Why does rain often cause flash flooding in the desert?
- What are some dangers you may face in the desert?
- Why do salt flats often form in the desert?
- Would you expect to find more salt flats in a cold desert or a hot desert?

THE SAHARA DESERT

The world's largest hot desert is the Sahara Desert in northern Africa. The Sahara is about the same size as the continental United States and larger than the continent of Australia. The Sahara Desert covers approximately 3,500,000 square miles (9,000,000 sq. km). It comprises parts of eleven different African countries and contains 25% of all of the sand in the world.

Because the Sahara Desert is so large, its climate and geography vary greatly from one area to another. Although all of the Sahara Desert is dry, the northern part of the desert is significantly hotter and dryer than the southern part. This desert contains miles and miles of sand dunes, but it also contains mountains, plateaus, and valleys. The highest point in the Sahara is Mt. Koussi in Chad, at an elevation of 11,204 feet (3,415 m). The lowest point in the Sahara is the Qattara Depression at an elevation of 436 feet below sea level (-133 m).

Within the borders of the Sahara Desert are several rivers. The primary river is the Nile River, flowing north through the Sahara into the Mediterranean Sea. There are also many salty lakes and one fresh lake—Lake Chad. So although the Sahara Desert is hot and dry, there are many areas of water throughout this amazing desert.

Although most of the Sahara desert is hot and dry today, we know that the climate in this area was significantly different in the past. Hundreds of petroglyphs exist showing many animals including crocodiles and elephants in areas that today do not have enough water to support that kind of life. Archaeologists have also discovered the remains of several towns in the desert where there is very little water today. Fossils of hippos and crocodiles have been found in the desert as well. Another clue comes from satellite views of the Sahara Desert, which show large river channels that are now dried up.

There are several proposed reasons for the dramatic change in climate, but the most likely explanation is that after the Flood, weather patterns and air flow were significantly different from today. The weather patterns after the Flood likely carried storms to the area that is now the Sahara Desert, bringing rainfall and allowing many animals and people to live in that area. After the oceans began to cool and ash from volcanoes began to clear, the weather changed to be more like what we see today, and the Sahara Desert no longer receives the rain it once did. In fact, today we see the desert actually growing. The southern border of the Sahara is moving south by as much as 30 miles (48 km) each year.

Extreme Ecosystems

OASES

A refreshing spot

Extreme Ecosystems

Why are oases important to people in the desert?

Words to know:

oasis

Swaying palm trees and cool shade might seem like a dream when you are in the middle of a desert; however, there are places in the desert that make that dream come true. An **oasis** is a special ecosystem located in a desert where there is abundant water. Usually this water comes from an underground spring. When the water table is high, wind may erode away enough sand to allow the water to bubble up to the surface, revealing a spring. Oases often occur along geographic fault lines, which allow the water table to be closer to the surface. Most deserts have several oases.

At an oasis, the water from the spring brings life. Many plants and animals that are naturally found in the desert are also found in the oasis; however, many other plants and animals are found at an oasis that are not normally found in the desert. In addition to cacti, lizards, snakes, and rodents, at an oasis you will find palm trees, shrubs, and grasses. These larger plants provide habitat for other animals such as bats, warblers, orioles, and robins. The water also provides habitat for fish and other aquatic life that do not live anywhere else in the desert.

In an oasis, the temperature can be as much as 10 to 20 degrees cooler than in the surrounding desert, so not only do you find shade from the sun, but the air temperature is actually cooler in an oasis. The air cools down in an oasis because of the increased evaporation taking place. The trees and other plants in an oasis perform photosynthesis. When they do this, they release water into the air through their leaves by transpiration. This water evaporates, removing energy from the air and thus cooling the air.

Travel through the desert can be very dangerous because of the heat and lack of water. Over hundreds of years, people have learned of and passed on the locations of oases so that they could travel safely across the desert. Trade routes sprang up from one oasis to another, and whoever controlled the oases often controlled the trade routes through the desert.

Some oases are very small with only a few trees and other plants growing around the spring. Other oases are much bigger with a large area that is watered by multiple springs. The Kharga oasis in the Sahara Desert is about 10 miles (16 km) long and from 12–50 miles (19–80 km) wide. This oasis has many springs and has been attracting people for hundreds of years. It contains a Persian monument dated from the 6th century BC as well as the ruins of several Roman forts. Today, the city of Kharga has about 60,000 residents and is about 100 miles (150 km) wide. It is a popular tourist attraction in southern Egypt. Las Vegas, Nevada began as an oasis in the desert. As the town outgrew the existing water supply, additional water has been brought in, but originally the town was an oasis in the desert.

The Imperial Valley in California is irrigated by the All-American Canal, which brings water from the Colorado River.

As in the cases of Kharga and Las Vegas, many desert oases have been expanded to create artificial oasis-type ecosystems in the deserts around the world. One of the most important man-made oases is the Imperial Valley in California. Although this area of southeastern California receives an average of only 3 inches (8 cm) of rain per year, it has become a very important agricultural area largely because of the All-American Canal which brings water from the Colorado River up to 80 miles (128 km) away. This water has turned the valley into a giant oasis. Similar canals are being used to turn parts of the desert in Israel into oases as well. Many of these canals are open to the air and much of the water evaporates before it ever reaches the farmland. However, some canals are being covered with plastic to help prevent unwanted evaporation.

The oasis is a unique ecosystem bringing refreshment and life to the hot dry desert. ■

TRANSPIRATION

Purpose: To observe transpiration

Materials: several plant leaves, plastic zipper bag

Procedure:

1. Place several plant leaves in a plastic zipper bag and seal the bag.

2. Place the bag in a sunny location for about 1 hour.

3. After 1 hour in the sun observe the bag. What do you see?

Conclusion:

You should see water condensing on the inside of the bag. Where did this water come from? The water was released from the leaves as they performed photosynthesis. In the dry desert air, the water from transpiration does not condense; instead, it evaporates and cools the air.

OASIS WORKSHEET

Complete the "Oasis" summary worksheet and add it to the desert section of your notebook. Find pictures of an oasis to include in your notebook.

WHAT DID WE LEARN?

- What is an oasis?
- What kinds of plants grow in an oasis?
- What kinds of animals live in an oasis that don't usually live in a desert?

TAKING IT FURTHER

- Why is it often cooler in an oasis than in a desert?
- Why are oases important for trade routes?
- How might a man-made oasis change the ecosystem in a desert?

PRODUCTS OF THE DESERT

People often think of the hot dry desert as a useless and lifeless place. You have already learned that there are many plants and animals in the desert, so you know it is not lifeless. The desert is also not useless. There are many things that make the desert a valuable place as well. Many important products come from deserts.

One of the most important products found in many deserts is petroleum. Significant amounts of oil have been found under the deserts in the Middle East, America, Australia, and Africa. The existence of petroleum in these desert areas is evidence of a very different climate in the past as well as evidence of the global Flood. Petroleum can be formed from marine organisms that have been buried and compressed. It is quite possible that much of the oil that exists today under the deserts

was formed as a result of the Genesis Flood.

Gold and diamonds are also found in several deserts. Deserts in Australia, Namibia, and South Africa contain some of the largest deposits of these precious materials. In fact, South Africa contains the world's largest diamond mines. The deserts in Australia are also a significant source of uranium, nickel, and aluminum. Deserts in Chile supply copper as well as sodium nitrate, which is used in making fertilizer.

One of the most abundant resources available in any desert is solar energy. Because of the lack of cloud cover, many deserts experience more than 300 days of sunshine per year. Many people are working to find ways to harness the sun's energy to help meet the energy needs of people around the world.

Do a little investigation of your own. Find out how the products of the desert are being used. Then, create a poster or report about desert products to include in your notebook.

FUN FACT

Several new solar power stations, each claiming to be the biggest solar energy station yet, are in the process of being built in the deserts of California, Nevada, and Arizona. These solar power stations are expected to save consumers millions of dollars and reduce carbon emissions by hundreds of tons each year.

Extreme Ecosystems

MOUNTAINS

Purple Mountain Majesties

LESSON 21

Why do mountains have different ecosystems at different altitudes?

Words to know:

timberline

snow line

Mountains are some of the most amazing geological formations in the world. They can tower thousands of feet above the surrounding landscape and be so beautiful they take your breath away. Mountains are found in every part of the world, even under the ocean. When an underwater mountain sticks up above the surface of the ocean we call it an island.

It is impossible to describe a single mountain ecosystem. Because most mountains are tall, the amount of light, wind, and precipitation changes as you gain altitude. The temperature also decreases with altitude. This creates varying ecosystems at different altitudes on a mountain.

Mountain ranges in temperate zones usually start with grasslands on the lowest parts of the mountains. As you go up, you will usually find deciduous forest ecosystems. These forests often contain beech, oak, basswood, maple and ash trees. Rhododendron and azalea plants also thrive in deciduous mountain forests.

At higher altitudes the deciduous trees give way to evergreen trees. At these higher altitudes the temperatures in the winter are often too cold and the climate is often too dry for many deciduous trees. Instead you find pine, spruce, fir, and juniper trees. Aspen trees are one of the few deciduous trees that do well at higher altitudes. These evergreen forests also contain cacti, and many wildflowers.

FUN FACT

Volcanoes are mountains. If the volcano has been inactive for a long time it may not seem different from other kinds of mountains. However, an active volcano has a constantly changing ecosystem.

As you continue going to higher altitudes, you reach a point where it is too cold and there is not enough air pressure for trees to grow. This point is called **timberline**. Above timberline, you will find the alpine meadows. Here you find shrubs, grasses and many mountain flowers such as columbine, larkspur, and glacier lily.

Above the alpine meadow the temperatures are very cold and the growing season is very short. This is where you find the alpine tundra. Only very small hardy plants can grow in the alpine tundra. Although the alpine tundra is similar in many ways to the Arctic tundra, it does not necessarily have the permafrost layer that the Arctic tundra has. Also, the animals found in the alpine tundra are different than in the Arctic tundra. You will not find polar bears or seals, but you will still find foxes, Arctic hares, and ground squirrels. You may also see small birds, insects, and pikas.

If you go even higher on a mountain, you eventually reach an altitude at which the snow no longer completely melts, even in the summertime. This is called the **snow line**. Because the snow does not completely melt above the snow line, there

are very few plants and only a few animals that visit the very highest peaks of these mountains.

The heights of mountains vary greatly from one location to another. So you will not find all the ecosystems listed above on every mountain. Many mountains, such as the Appalachian Mountains are primarily deciduous forest. Many areas of the Rocky Mountains start at 5,000 feet above sea level, so they begin with evergreen forests. Only a small percentage of mountains are tall enough to have a permanent cover of snow, so many mountains do not have a snow line. Nevertheless, you usually find more than one ecosystem on a mountain.

The animals that live in the mountains often move between ecosystems by moving up and down the mountain. However, many animals live primarily in one or two ecosystems. Animals you are likely to find in mountain ecosystems include bears, timber wolves, mountain lions, porcupines, chipmunks, hummingbirds, bluebirds, and eagles. Above timberline you often find pikas, marmots, big horned sheep, and mountain goats. Animals such as sheep and goats are well suited for the rocky terrain of many mountain areas. They have split hooves with soft flexible pads. This allows them to cling to the changing surfaces of the mountains, making them great climbers.

Mountain ranges in northern areas were greatly influenced by glaciers. The glaciers that covered much of North America during the Ice Age helped to carve out many of the valleys and mountain lakes in the United States and Canada. Some glaciers still exist on high mountaintops. These glaciers feed many of the streams and lakes in the summertime.

Mountains in tropical zones also experience various ecosystems as you gain altitude, but the ecosystems are somewhat different than in temperate zones. Often tropical mountains have rainforests near the bottom of the mountain. Then as you go up, the rainforest gives way to bamboo forest. Above the bamboo forest is the heath, which is an ecosystem composed of a variety of shrubs. At higher altitudes you find areas of small plants and flowers and above that you find alpine tundra. ▪

MOUNTAIN WORKSHEET

Complete the "Mountain" summary worksheet and add it to your notebook. Find pictures of plants and animals that live in various ecosystems on mountains to include in your notebook.

MODELING A MOUNTAIN

Purpose: To demonstrate the diverse ecosystems found on a mountainside

Materials: art supplies, newspaper, paint, twigs, leaves, grass, small flowers, cotton balls

Procedure:

1. Form newspaper into the shape of a mountain.

2. Paint your mountain with greens and browns to represent grass and rocks on the side of the mountain. Allow the paint to dry.

3. Use whatever materials you have to glue to the sides of your mountain to represent the different ecosystems you might encounter as you go up the mountain. Use your imagination. Here are some ideas to help get you started:

   a. Glue grass near the bottom to represent grassland.

   b. Glue leaves and twigs higher up to represent forests.

   c. Glue small flowers higher up to represent alpine meadows or tundra.

   d. Stretch out and glue cotton balls near the top to represent snow.

   e. Use any other materials you have available.

4. Take a picture of your mountain and include it in your notebook with an explanation of each ecosystem that is represented.

Conclusion:

Mountains are rich with diversity of plant and animal life. You can enjoy several different ecosystems in one day just by visiting the mountains.

WHAT DID WE LEARN?

- What ecosystems are you likely to encounter on mountains in temperate zones?
- What ecosystems are you likely to encounter on mountains in tropical zones?
- What is timberline?
- What is snow line?

TAKING IT FURTHER

- Why do the ecosystems change as you gain altitude on a mountain?
- Why don't you find every ecosystem on every mountain?
- What other ecosystems are you likely to find on mountains that were not listed in this lesson?
- How have glaciers influenced the shapes of mountains?
- Why is there less oxygen as you gain altitude?

Extreme Ecosystems

THE HIMALAYAS

Extreme Ecosystems

The highest mountain range in the world is the Himalayan Range, often just called the Himalayas. This mountain range is actually three parallel ranges that stretch 1,500 miles (2,400 km) between the Indian subcontinent and the Tibetan Plateau of Asia. This mountain range is home to 100 peaks that are over 23,000 feet (7,200 m) high.

As you would expect, with the Himalayas covering such a large area of land, the mountains have many different ecosystems. These ecosystems change not only with altitude, but also from west to east. The amount of rainfall increases as you move from west to east, so the ecosystems change as well. The snow line also changes from east to west and from north to south. In some areas the snow line is as low as 14,100 feet (4,300 km). In other areas the snow line is as high as 19,700 feet (6,000 km).

At the lowest altitudes are the Lowlands. This is an area of forest found at the base of most of the mountains. As you gain altitude you enter the Teri belt, which is an area of mostly grasslands. These are some of the highest grasslands in the world. Above this are the Midlands. In the west the Midlands consist of temperate deciduous forests. In the east they consist mostly of pine forests. As you go up you encounter alpine meadows and alpine tundra. Finally, since so many of the mountains in the Himalayas are so tall, most of them have glaciers at the top. In fact, there are over 15,000 glaciers in the Himalayas.

Obviously with so many ecosystems, the Himalayas are home to large numbers of different plant and animal species. Some of the animals that are unique to the Himalayas include the snow leopard, clouded leopard, Bengal tiger, and red panda. You also find many common mountain animals such as deer, goats, sheep, wolves, and marmots.

The highest mountain in the world, Mount Everest, is found in the Himalayas. It towers up at 29,035 feet (8,848 m) with K2 not far behind at 28,251 feet (8,611 m). The weather on the tops of these high mountains is very unpredictable and very dangerous. Only a small number of people have ever successfully scaled these heights. Sir Edmond Hillary and Tenzing Norgay were the first people to reach the summit of Mount Everest on May 23, 1953. K2 was first successfully scaled in 1954. At these extreme heights, there is very little oxygen and climbers must carry oxygen tanks with them. No plants and few animals are found at these altitudes.

The Himalayas are very important to the climate and well being of the Indian subcontinent. First, the Himalayas provide a barrier for the monsoon moisture that sweeps inland from the Indian Ocean. This causes much of that moisture to fall in the mountains. This water then drains into three major river systems that carry the water to the 1.3 billion people that live on the Indian subcontinent. These rivers not only provide water, but also wash down tons of silt which enriches the soil of the plains and valleys fed by the rivers.

There is much more to learn about the Himalayas. Choose an area that interests you and find out more about it. Then take what you have learned and make a Himalayas page for your notebook.

CHAPARRAL

The Mediterranean climate

LESSON 22

Where does the word *chaparral* come from?

Words to know:

chaparral

Challenge words:

fire cues

The Spanish word for scrub oak is *chaparral*, and the **chaparral** is an ecosystem that is unique to hot, dry mountain slopes that are often filled with shrubs. The chaparral is found in semi-arid climates in California, around the Mediterranean Sea, and in Australia. It is sometimes called the Mediterranean ecosystem or maquis (mah-KEE). In a chaparral, the summer days are warm and sunny and the winters are mild and rainy.

As the name would imply, the chaparral is dominated by shrubs. These plants usually grow in very dense thickets. Sometimes these thickets are so thick that large mammals and even people cannot penetrate them. Common plants in the chaparral include scrub oak, live oak, yucca, buckbrush, and lotus. In many areas of chaparral, citrus fruit trees and grapes are cultivated by farmers.

Because most large mammals cannot move about in the chaparral, the wildlife is mostly smaller animals. In the chaparral you will find woodrats, brush rabbits, gray foxes, coyotes, bob-cats, quail, blue jays, wrens, and sparrows. Where the foliage is less dense you may find some deer as well. In the chaparral in Australia you commonly find eucalyptus trees and koalas. In areas along the Mediterranean Sea you also find many goats and other climbing animals.

Summers are hot and dry in the chaparral.

FUN FACT

Chaps are special coverings worn by many cowboys to protect their legs. The name chaps comes from the word chaparral. Cowboys needed protection from the thick shrubbery when riding through the chaparral.

CHAPARRAL WORKSHEET

Complete the "Chaparral" summary worksheet and add it to the mountains section of your notebook. Find pictures of plants and animals that live in the chaparral to include in your notebook.

FIRE IN THE CHAPARRAL

Find pictures of the chaparral before a fire, shortly after a fire, and several years after a fire. Use these pictures to make a page about the effects of fire in the chaparral for your notebook.

Summertime temperatures often reach 104°F (40°C) with very little rainfall. In the winter the daytime temperatures average 50°F (10°C) with 15–40 inches (38–100 cm) of rainfall per year.

Because summers are hot and dry, and because the shrubs are so dense, wildfires are very common in the chaparral. Lightning strikes are the most common cause of these fires. Low humidity and high winds help the fires to spread and become very large. Although this may seem like a devastating event for an ecosystem, God has designed the plants in the chaparral to recover after a wildfire just as they do in the grasslands. New seeds will quickly sprout and areas that were burned will soon be growing and thriving again. Some species that grow in the chaparral cannot germinate unless they experience a fire. In fact, in areas where there has not been a fire for more than 10–15 years, some species begin to die out from overcrowding and inability to germinate.

Wildfires, particularly in southern California, cause many problems for the people that live in the chaparral. Although the fires may be good for the ecosystem, they are not good for people's houses. There is a constant battle each summer against these fires in an effort to protect people's homes and businesses. ■

A wildfire in southern California

FIRE GERMINATION

Several species of plants that live in the chaparral only germinate when their seeds experience a fire. Some of these plants include scrub oak, ceanthus, toyon, manzanita, and holly-leafed cherry. Although it is known that many of these seeds will not germinate unless they experience a fire, it is not completely clear why or how a fire triggers germination.

Many experiments have been done to try to understand the role that fire plays in the germination of many of these seeds. It is believed that there are several different types of fire cues, or conditions, which could cause a seed to germinate. The most obvious cue is heat. When a fire sweeps through an area the ground can experience temperatures of several hundred degrees. It is believed that some seeds need high temperature to trigger germination.

A second fire cue is smoke. Scientists believe that some seeds need to experience smoke from a fire before they will germinate. Tests have been conducted that put aerosols into the air. Other tests have dissolved smoke in water. Both airborne smoke and dissolved smoke have been shown to trigger germination in some seeds.

Other fire cues include charred wood, oxidation due to burning, and adding of acids to the soil during a fire. All of these cues have been shown to be effective in trig-

A manzanita bush

gering germination in some species. Although there are many different cues, it is clear that God designed many of these species to survive and repopulate the area after a fire.

Extreme Ecosystems

CAVES

Are they just holes in the ground?

Extreme Ecosystems

What will you find in a cave?

Words to know:

cave

trogloxene

troglophile

troglobite

guano

chemosynthesis

Challenge words:

echolocation

Have you ever been inside a real cave? Did you have a flashlight or other source of light with you? You probably needed it because a cave is a dark place. A **cave** is a cavern inside a mountain or underground. A true cave has no light except at the entrance to the cave. Because there is no light in a cave there are no green plants in a cave. There may be a few small plants or some algae growing at the entrance, but once you actually get inside a cave there are no plants. This greatly limits the food supply in a cave, so a cave is considered a low energy ecosystem. In general, it is relatively difficult to explore most caves, so very little is known about their ecosystems.

We know that there are three major groups of animals in a cave ecosystem. The first group is called **trogloxenes**. These are the animals that visit the cave but do not spend most of their lives in the cave. Raccoons and woodrats are examples of animals that may be found in a cave at a given period of time, but do not spend most of their time there. The most famous of the trogloxenes is the bat. Bats spend the day roosting inside the cave, but they leave every night in search of food and return at dawn. Many bats only spend certain seasons in caves, and some bats roost in trees or man-made structures instead of in caves.

The second group of animals is the **troglophiles**. These are animals that like to live in the cave, often near the entrance. Similar animals may be found living outside of caves. These animals often leave the cave in search of food and then return to the cave. Salamanders, millipedes, and snails are examples of animals that spend most of their time in the cave but periodically leave and then return. Some scientists group bats with the troglophiles instead of with the trogloxenes.

Troglobites are animals that live in the cave their entire lives. They live in complete darkness and many of them have very little or no pigment. Some of them are completely blind. Since there is no light in a cave, these animals have no need for eyesight. However, many of these animals have a heightened sense of hearing or other senses that help them to survive in the darkness. Crayfish, shrimp, crickets, fish, and scorpions are animals you may find in the darkest parts of a cave.

Since there are no plants inside a cave, you may be wondering what the animals eat. Obviously, the animals that live near the entrance can go out of the cave to get food. But the animals that spend their entire lives inside the cave must also have something to eat. Some organic material—parts of dead plants or animals—gets washed into the cave when it rains or gets blown in by the wind, providing food for some of the animals. Some animals are predators and eat other animals that live in the cave. But the greatest source of nutrients for the animals in the cave is bat **guano**, or bat droppings.

The bats get their food from outside the cave, but spend a significant portion of their lives roosting in the caves, often leaving a thick layer of guano on the floor of the cave. Bacteria and fungi in the cave eat the guano and excrete nutrients that are eaten by other animals such as the crickets. The crickets then become food for the larger animals such as crayfish and scorpions.

Another source of food has been found in one cave in Romania. Scientists have found a certain kind of bacteria living in this cave that can use sulfur, rather than sunlight, to produce carbon-based molecules, thus providing food for the other animals. This process is called **chemosynthesis** and is uncommon. Chemosynthesis also takes place near the thermal vents on the bottom of the ocean where there is no light available.

The amount of life in caves is very low compared to other ecosystems. There are three main limiting factors that keep life from flourishing. First, there is a limited food supply. This limits how many animals can survive. Second, the temperature must be fairly constant for the animals to survive. This is related to the food supply. If the temperature rises inside the cave, the cold-blooded animals' body temperatures increase. With a higher body temperature and higher metabolism the animals will now need more food, which may not be available. Finally, humidity is also a limiting

CAVE WORKSHEET

Complete the "Cave" summary worksheet and add it to the mountain section of your notebook. Find interesting pictures of cave formations as well as animals to include in your notebook.

PLANTS IN CAVES?

Purpose: To understand why plants don't live in caves

Materials: houseplant, box

Procedure:

1. Place a box over the top of a houseplant. Be sure that the box completely covers the plant and does not allow any light inside.

2. Each day, lift the box and water the plant just enough to make the soil moist without making it soggy. It would be best to do this at night when there is no sunlight.

3. Observe the plant each day for several days. How does it look after 1 week with no sunlight?

Conclusion:

Green plants require sunlight to perform photosynthesis and grow. Without sunlight, plants will die. Inside a cave there is no sunlight so no green plants can grow there.

factor in the amount of life found in a cave. When a cave dries out, animals such as salamanders dry out, too. This causes many of them to die.

Although cave life is somewhat fragile and is certainly unusual, the fact that life exists there at all is testimony to God's creative power. ■

WHAT DID WE LEARN?

- What is a cave?
- What kinds of plants will you find in a cave ecosystem?
- What are the three categories of animals in a cave ecosystem?
- Explain the different habits of each category of cave animal.
- What is the main source of nutrients in a cave ecosystem?

TAKING IT FURTHER

- Why is a cave considered a low energy ecosystem?
- Why can a rise in temperature inside a cave threaten the ecosystem?
- Which sense is least useful in a cave?
- Which senses are most useful in a cave?

BATS

The most important animal in most cave ecosystems is the bat. Bats are very interesting animals. They are the only mammals that truly fly. The wings of a bat are actually thin membranes of skin stretched between very long, slender fingers. There are also membranes connecting the hind feet with the tail for a complete wingspan.

Most bats eat insects; however, some bats eat fruit, fish, or even blood. Bats that eat insects usually have poor eyesight, but have good hearing. They also are able to hunt using echolocation. Echolocation is similar to sonar used on submarines. The bat sends out a high frequency sound wave. The sound bounces off of things around it and the bat can detect the reflected waves. This

helps the bat create a mental picture of its surroundings. Echolocation works so well that bats can quickly navigate through completely dark caves and snatch insects out of the air while flying.

The most common insect-eating bat in North America is the brown bat. These bats roost in trees or buildings during the summer, but spend their winters in caves. Another insect-eating bat is the Brazilian free-tailed bat, which winters in Mexico and spends the summers in the southern United States. These bats collect by the thousands and roost in the famous Carlsbad Caverns in New Mexico.

The smallest insect-eating bat is the Kitti's hog-nosed bat. It is only 1 inch (2.5cm) long and lives in caves in the rainforests.

The largest bat is the fruit bat, often called the flying fox because of its long pointed face. Its body is up to 16 inches (40 cm) long and it can have a wing span up to 6 feet (1.8 m). Fruit-eating bats do not use echolocation to find their food. Instead, they have very keen eyesight

and can see the fruit. They also listen for the sounds emitted by other bats to help them locate food. Most fruit bats roost in the trees of swamps and forests instead of in caves.

Fruit bats present an interesting problem for evolutionists. Many scientists looking at the very sharp teeth of the bat would assume that it had sharp teeth because it was a carnivore. However, fruit bats eat only fruit. They use their sharp teeth to penetrate the fruit and extract the juice, not to eat meat. This shows that God's design does not always match man's expectations.

The fisherman bat eats fish. It flies low over a river or lake and snatches fish from the water with its hind feet. It may eat the fish while it is flying or take it back to its roost to eat. Like most bats, the fisherman bat is nocturnal and generally hunts at night. Other bats eat frogs and other small animals.

The most frightening bat may be the vampire bat. Vampire bats seldom feed on people, but because they get their nourishment from the blood of other animals, people often

fear them. Vampire bats usually eat the blood of large mammals such as cattle or horses. The bat lands near the animal and uses its wings to move across the ground. Then the bat makes an incision with its teeth. The bat then uses its tongue to lap up to two teaspoons of blood from the animal. This does not usually harm the animal; however, since bats can carry diseases such as rabies, the incision runs the risk of spreading diseases.

While some bats migrate to warmer climates in the winter, many bats hibernate. They will find a cave and sleep while hanging upside down (see photo). Bats can hang upside down for extended periods of time because God designed them to be able to do this. There are tendons attached from the bat's feet to its upper body, so when its body pulls down, the tendons naturally cause the toes to squeeze shut without the bat having to exert any effort. Also, its circulatory system is designed to keep the blood from rushing to the bat's head when it is hanging upside down. The bat is most at rest when hanging upside down.

Bats are amazing creatures and are vital to the health of a cave ecosystem. Use what you have learned about bats and make a page about bats to include in your notebook.

FUN FACT

A brown bat can eat as many as 600 mosquitoes in one hour.

5

UNIT ANIMAL BEHAVIORS

SEASONAL BEHAVIORS

It happens every year.

How do the seasons affect animals?

Words to know:

hibernation

migration

Challenge words:

animal courtship

Because of the tilt of the earth with respect to the sun, most parts of the earth experience different seasons. Summers are warmer than winters in nearly every part of the earth. The change in seasons triggers some very interesting behavior in many animals. Scientists believe the change in the number of hours of daylight is the primary factor in many of these behaviors.

In areas with very cold winters, many animals hibernate. **Hibernation** is a state in which the animal goes into a very deep sleep. The animal's heart rate and breathing slow down significantly and its body temperature drops. A hibernating animal does not wake up to eat; it survives the hibernation by using up fat stored in its body. A hibernating animal's metabolism may be so slow that it may actually appear dead to the casual observer. This slow state allows the animal to spend the winter in a burrow protected from the harsh environment and sleep until the weather becomes more favorable. When the daylight hours start lengthening, the animal wakes up and begins searching for food.

Bats, squirrels, woodchucks, and different insects are some of the many animals that hibernate. Some people think that bears hibernate as well. Many bears do spend much of the winter in a deep sleep; however, the bear's metabolism does not significantly slow down and it can awaken and search for food in the middle of winter. So bears do not experience true hibernation. In deserts, many animals sleep through the summer to avoid the hot dry weather. This is called estivation,

FUN FACT

The Arctic tern has the longest migration of any animal. It flies 25,000 miles (40,000 km) each way when it migrates. It flies from pole to pole.

Animal Behaviors

MONARCH BUTTERFLIES

The migration of the monarch butterfly is very fascinating. The butterflies start out in the northern United States and in Canada. In the fall, as the days become shorter, the butterflies begin their long journey south. Monarchs that are east of the Rocky Mountains fly to southern Mexico while those west of the Rocky Mountains fly to southern California. They stop to eat along the way, but also use fat stored in their abdomens for additional energy. When they reach their destination, the butterflies hibernate for the winter.

When the days get longer in the spring, the butterflies begin heading north again. Along the way, they mate and lay eggs. The butterflies that spent the winter in the south usually die before returning to their original homes. Their offspring hatch and turn into butterflies within a few weeks. These new butterflies continue the trip north. When they reach the northern point of their journey, this second generation mates and lays eggs and then dies in the north. Their offspring hatch in late summer and, after changing into butterflies, begin the journey south that their grandparents made the year before.

Scientists are not sure how these grandchildren, and sometimes great grandchildren, know where to go during their migration. But they have determined that the butterflies return to the same areas, and sometimes even the same trees that were inhabited by the previous generations. God has given them the instinctive ability to return to their winter roosting grounds, having never been there before.

Do some research on the migration of monarch butterflies and make a map showing the routes of each generation. Include this map in your notebook in the animal behaviors section.

and is a similar state to hibernation, only it occurs in the summer.

Another way that many animals deal with changing seasons and unfavorable weather is by **migration**, the moving from one area to another for a particular season. Although we usually think of bird migrations, other animals such as sea turtles, whales, and butterflies also migrate. Again, migration is usually triggered by the changing number of daylight hours. Animals generally migrate to find better food supplies, milder weather, and often for reproduction.

Most animals that migrate move from north to south and back again. The animals move toward the equator in the wintertime and back toward the poles in the summertime. However, in some areas, such as in parts of Europe, animals migrate from east to west. Some animals move from the mainland to the British Isles during the winter because Great Britain usually has milder winters than most of Europe. Then the animals return to the mainland in the summer.

Migrating is a very complex behavior. Not only do the animals know when to leave an area, but they often travel thousands of miles during each trip without getting lost. A particular bird often returns to the same nesting area each year after traveling thousands of miles. Scientists are not sure how these animals navigate. They believe that some animals use the stars as a reference. This certainly seems to be the case with sea turtles as well as with some birds. Other birds seem to use landmarks to help guide them, and some are believed to use the earth's magnetic field lines. Fish and other aquatic animals often use smell to help them find their way.

Birds generally fly to their summer and winter homes. Flying requires a great deal of energy. Most birds spend time building up stores of fat before migrating so they will have the required energy. Many birds stop periodically and eat, so they do not have to have enough body fat for the entire journey, but the Golden Plover flies 2,000 miles (3,200 km) non-stop over water and must have enough energy for the entire flight. God has amazingly designed this bird to make the flight without dying.

Birds generally migrate in flocks and often fly in a V-shaped formation. This is because the *V* formation is a very efficient way to fly. This formation breaks up the air currents and reduces friction. The lead bird has the most difficult time, so migrating birds take turns being the leader. In North America there are four distinct migratory flyways that different species of birds use. They are the Pacific, central, Mississippi, and Atlantic flyways. Within each flyway, particular species of birds seem to have their own corridors in which they fly.

Although most migration is seasonal, some migrations happen only once. Pacific salmon are born in rivers. They swim to the ocean where they spend most of their lives. Then, when it is time for them to mate, they swim back up stream to the exact place where they were born. There they reproduce and then die. Their migration is a once-in-a-lifetime experience. Scientists believe that the fish use their sensitive sense of smell to follow the right path to their spawning grounds in the river where they were born.

When you look at the complex patterns of migration and the abilities of animals to hibernate and estivate, you see the hand of a wonderful Creator. God has designed these animals to survive the changing seasons. ■

Salmon migrate to the exact place they were born where they reproduce and then die.

WHAT DID WE LEARN?

- What is hibernation?
- What is estivation?
- What is migration?
- List three different kinds of animals that migrate.
- What is the most likely trigger for seasonal behaviors?

TAKING IT FURTHER

- How can animals know where they are supposed to go when they migrate if they have never been there before?
- How do animals navigate while migrating?
- Why might a group of animals move from one location to another, other than for their annual migration?
- If you see a monarch butterfly in the fall and then see another one in the spring, how likely is it that you are seeing the same butterfly?

ANIMAL COURTSHIP

Animal Behaviors

Springtime brings many changes in the wildlife in most areas. The migrating birds return and begin their songs. The plants begin growing again after their winter rest. And many animals begin courtship. Animal courtship is a way for animals to attract mates. Some species mate for life and only go through their courtship process once. Other species choose new mates each year. The courtship rituals are as varied as the animals themselves, but they all serve the same purpose. The male demonstrates his superiority over other males so the female will be willing to choose him, and his competition will back off.

Birds have some of the most creative and interesting courtship rituals. The Bird of Paradise does an elaborate dance as part of its courtship ritual. The male peacock spreads it brightly colored tail feathers in a brilliant display to impress the ladies. The red crowned crane not only prances around with a stiff neck, but it also tosses sticks and grass around and sings a duet with its prospective mate. The male sage grouse has inflatable neck sacs which he uses to amplify the plopping noises he makes as he courts the females. These sacs make the noises loud enough to be heard up to three miles away. The male bowerbird

builds an elaborate structure and struts around in front of it to attract a female.

Many animals other than birds also have courtship rituals. The hissing cockroach hisses and rubs the potential mate's antennae. The pink dolphin, which lives in the Amazon River, presents stones to a potential mate. Elk make loud bugling noises to attract a mate. In addition, male elk may fight each other using their massive antlers to prove their strength and ability to mate with the females they have attracted.

Many courtship rituals involve sounds and elaborate shows, but other animals are more subtle. They produce chemicals called pheromones which attract the opposite sex of the same species. These chemical scents may be on the animal itself or may be spread by the animal onto plants in its area. This smell advertises to anyone in the area that the animal is looking for a mate.

Many courtships take place in the spring, with babies being born later that year. However, some courtships take place in the fall or other times of the year depending on the species. Most birds mate in the spring, but elk mate in the fall. Regardless of the time of year, the changing seasons are still the trigger for the courtship behavior. This behavior helps to ensure that the animals find a mate and are able to reproduce.

ANIMAL DEFENSES

A matter of protection

How do animals protect themselves?

Words to know:

camouflage

Challenge words:

dormant

Before the Fall of man in the Garden of Eden, animals did not prey on one another. All animals ate plants and there was no death. But after man sinned, God cursed the earth. Part of the Curse includes the fact that many animals now survive by eating other animals. However, God did not make the prey totally defenseless. Animals have many ways that they can defend themselves against their attackers. Most of these defenses can be grouped into three types: flight, trickery, or fight.

The first instinct of most animals when they feel threatened is to run away. Some animals are much faster than their predators and can use that speed as their main defense. Deer and other grazing animals are usually fast runners and can outrun many of their predators. Other animals can dive into burrows or quickly hide to get away from predators. Some animals such as antelope and prairie dogs post guards to watch for trouble. When they sense danger, they signal an alarm so the herd or colony can retreat to safety. Prairie dogs are well known for their barking alarm that is passed from one part of the colony to another to warn of approaching danger.

Trickery is also widely used by animals as defense techniques. One of the most effective defenses is **camouflage**. Many animals can blend in with their surroundings, making it difficult for predators to find them. Chameleons can change the color of their skin to match their surroundings. Many insects are shaped to resemble sticks, leaves, or other things in their environment, making them difficult to spot. Tigers, leopards, and other animals are multi-colored, which breaks up their shape and helps them blend in. Other animals, such as the Arctic fox and Arctic hare turn white in the winter when the ground is covered with snow, and others have fur or feathers that help them match the colors of their surroundings.

ANIMAL DEFENSES

Purpose: To create a card game that will help you appreciate the many ways that animals can defend themselves

Materials: card stock or tag board, drawing materials, pictures of animals

Procedure:

1. Cut several sheets of card stock into identical pieces to make a deck of cards.

2. Make pairs of cards. One card should have a picture of an animal. The other card should have a description of its defense. Be sure that the defense is specific enough that it only applies to one particular animal in your deck. Following are several ideas for card pairs. Use these and as many of your own ideas as you like.

3. When you have all of your cards made, you can play a matching game by mixing up the cards then spreading them on the table face down. Take turns turning over two cards to try to make a match. When you make a match you get to keep the cards and take another turn. If you do not make a match, turn the cards back over, and it becomes the next person's turn.

4. Take a picture of your cards when they are spread out face up and include the picture in your notebook.

Ideas for cards

Prairie dog—Bark to alert colony

Tiger—Stripes for camouflage

Arctic fox—White fur for camouflage

Chameleon—Changes color

Gorilla—Beats its chest for intimidation

Puffer fish—Fills its body with air

Rattlesnake—Rattles on its tail

Poison dart frog—Body covered with poison

Stick bug—Looks like a stick

Octopus—Shoots ink

In addition to camouflage, many animals try to trick their enemies into leaving them alone by their behavior. Some animals try to intimidate their attackers into leaving them alone. The male mountain gorilla will stand up on its hind legs and beat its chest. It also growls and bares its teeth. This aggressive behavior often encourages enemies to back off. Many other animals will bark, growl, or yelp to warn predators to stay away. The puffer fish can fill itself with air, making it seem much bigger than it actually is and making it difficult for its enemy to get a good grip on it.

Another way that animals try to confuse their enemies is by squirting out ink. Octopi and squids can shoot out a cloud of ink to hide their movements; allowing them to make a quick get away. The regal horned lizard can actually shoot blood out of its eyes to frighten away its enemies.

Most animals prefer to either get away from their enemies or to frighten their enemies away. But even when these defenses do not work, most animals have some way to protect themselves. Many

The porcupine has hundreds of sharp quills which discourage anyone from taking a bite.

have horns, antlers, claws, or teeth with which to fight. The porcupine has hundreds of sharp quills which discourage anyone from taking a bite. Some animals, such as the electric eel, can give a nasty electrical shock to a predator. Others coat themselves in nasty tasting chemicals and some even have poisonous bites with which they defend themselves.

Although the animals were not originally created to need these defense mechanisms, they were designed by God with the ability to develop these defenses. Predators also have developed ways to enable them to capture their prey so they do not starve. This struggle is part of the Curse, but still shows God's provision for the continuance of life for both the predator and the prey. ■

WHAT DID WE LEARN?

- What are three main ways that animals try to defend themselves?
- List three ways that animals can trick their enemies into leaving them alone.
- How do some eels protect themselves?

TAKING IT FURTHER

- Why do you think animals prefer to run away or frighten off enemies rather than fight?
- Why do many animals prefer trickery to running away?
- How might a defense also serve as an attack method?

PLANT DEFENSES

Animals are not the only organisms that are able to defend themselves. Many plants also have defenses. Most plants are easy food for the animals that rely on them. We have already seen how grass was designed by God to grow quickly even when it is being eaten regularly. However, because of the Curse, may plants live in harsh conditions. Since the Fall they too have to struggle for survival. Many of these plants have defense mechanisms that help them to survive.

Many desert plants have sharp needles, which discourage animals from eating them. Other plants have thorns, which also discourage animals from eating them. Some plants put out chemicals that prevent other plants from growing too closely to them. This prevents other plants from competing with them for water, sunlight, and nutrients in the soil.

Other plant defenses are not defenses against animals or other plants; instead, they are defenses against the harsh weather. The most common defense against the cold is for plants to shed their leaves in the fall and go **dormant** during the winter. Other plants go dormant when there is not enough water. Dormancy is a plant defense.

Just like with animals, plants did not need these defenses in God's original creation. There, growing conditions were just right—there were no thorns or thistles. But after the Fall, even the plants were cursed and now have to struggle to survive.

ADAPTATION

Fitting in

How do animals change?

Words to know:

adaptation

survival of the fittest

natural selection

Challenge words:

adaptive radiation

Have you ever had something unexpected happen and you had to adapt to the situation? Maybe a storm suddenly came up and you needed an umbrella; or perhaps you had unexpected visitors and you had to change your plans for the day. However, this is not the way we speak of adaptation in nature. Plants and animals have been designed with special adaptations. **Adaptations** are physical traits or behaviors that allow an organism to be better suited to a given environment.

Adaptation is a word that is greatly misused and misunderstood. Evolutionary scientists say that an organism has adapted to its environment by developing new traits over time. These new traits make it better suited for where it lives. Waterfowl have webbed feet making them good swimmers. Birds' feathers have a hook and barb design making them easy to repair and good for flying. Perching birds have toes that go both directions on their feet, making them good for grasping branches. Creation scientists believe these are design features created by God.

Scientists also refer to differences between two similar species as adaptations. Some squirrels are grey and others are brown, depending on which kinds of trees they are likely to live in. Polar bears are white and have slightly

DESIGN WORKSHEET

Complete the "How Was I Designed?" worksheet and include it in your notebook. For each plant or animal that is listed, describe one or more design features it has that make it adapted or well-suited to its particular environment.

webbed feet, which makes them better able to survive in the Arctic than their cousins, the brown bears, that live in the Rocky Mountains. Pink dolphins are able to live in freshwater, and bottlenose dolphins live in salty water. These differences between similar species can be used to show that animals have characteristics that are related to their niches and their environment.

Evolutionists claim that adaptations, such as webbed feet in ducks, are the result of changes in an organism over time as they evolved from one kind of organism into another (originally coming from a single-celled ancestor). But the Bible says that God created distinct kinds of animals. Ducks were always ducks and were designed with webbed feet from the very beginning. Webbed feet are not adaptations. The foot structure may change slightly over time, but it did not come from a claw.

Adaptations represent real changes that we see between different species of the same kind of animal. This is the result of the process of adaptation. So, how do animals change to adapt to their environment? Chance mutations cause a creature to have slightly different characteristics from the others of its kind. If this characteristic is beneficial, that creature survives better than the others and is likely to pass this characteristic on to the next generation, making its offspring more likely to survive and reproduce as well. This is referred to as **survival of the fittest**, or **natural selection**. Evolutionists claim that these mutations add new characteristics and take long periods of time, perhaps millions of years, to become well established. Eventually, enough mutations cause changes and a lizard has evolved into a duck.

However, the Bible says that all animals were created just 6,000 years ago as distinct kinds with great variety in their DNA. After the Fall, mutations and other genetic mechanisms also altered the DNA. After the Flood, animals left the Ark reproducing and spreading out across the earth. Their offspring had great variety.

As the animals moved to different parts of the earth, the environments were different, and those with advantageous characteristics for a particular environment were the ones to survive and have offspring. This is natural selection; however, this does not require new characteristics to be added through genetic mutation. Instead, it accepts the fact that God designed the animals with the ability to produce many different characteristics. The variety is the result of the original DNA being recombined in new ways as well as being altered by mutations. Natural selection simply acts on the traits that are already present—it does not make new traits in the population. These changes in populations do not require millions of years to happen, but can take place in only a few generations as existing characteristics are modified.

The characteristics that make organisms suited for the environments in which they live are designed characteristics or modifications of the traits that already existed. They are not the result of evolution. ■

WHAT DID WE LEARN?

- What is adaptation?
- Are all helpful characteristics a result of a change in the organism?
- What process causes different species to develop among the same kind of animal or plant?

TAKING IT FURTHER

- How does natural selection work?
- Does natural selection require millions of years to develop distinct populations?
- Does natural selection require genetic mutation?

DARWIN'S FINCHES

One of the most famous examples of adaptation is found among the Galapagos Island finches, sometimes called Darwin's finches. These birds were observed by Charles Darwin and the other scientists aboard the HMS Beagle in the 1830s. At first Darwin thought there were several different kinds of birds, but after much examination it was determined that there were actually 13 different species of finches that had likely developed from one original type of finch. This process of developing different species from a common ancestor is called adaptive radiation.

The biggest difference between the various species of finches is in the size and shape of their beaks. Some of the finches have long, narrow beaks. Others have short, wide beaks. Others have hooked beaks. The dominant type of beak in the community seems to depend on the food that is most readily available on the different islands. Some birds eat leaves, others eat fruits and buds. Some eat insects, while others eat grubs or seeds. The beak that each species has is suited for the kind of food that is available in that area.

It is believed that a single kind of finch arrived in the Galapagos Islands. Their offspring spread out among the islands. The original pair had the genetic ability to produce offspring with many different shapes and sizes of beaks. In each area, the offspring that had the best kind of beak for the available food supplies were more successful in surviving and reproducing, so eventually all of the offspring on a particular island had the preferred kind of beak for that particular area.

Darwin and other evolutionists claim that this natural selection required millions of years to develop. Evolutionists claim that the differences in beaks have come about because of genetic mutations and therefore long periods of time are required for enough mutations to take place. However, modern research in the Galapagos Islands has shown that long periods of time are not required.

Researchers, like Peter and Rosemary Grant, have been studying the finches in the Galapagos since 1973. They have recorded the climatic changes that have affected the food available in different areas. They have shown that the changes in climate can cause changes in available food supplies, and have also shown that the species that are dominant can change very quickly, within only a few generations. Millions of years are not required for the dominant species to change.

Although Darwin's finches are a great example of adaptation and natural selection, they do not demonstrate evolution. They show that a creative God made finches with a wide variety of possible characteristics and that particular characteristics become dominant in certain environments, but they do not show that a finch changed into anything other than a finch. The finches also do not demonstrate any possible mechanism for one organism to change into different kinds of organisms. So although you may see claims that Darwin's finches prove evolution, you can be sure that they do not. They actually support what the Bible has said all along.

Animal Behaviors

BALANCE OF NATURE

Keeping it working

How do populations stay in balance?

Words to know:

balance of nature

predator-prey feedback loop

territoriality

Challenge words:

GMO—genetically modified organism

Have you ever seen a gymnast perform on a balance beam? She has to keep in the middle without going too far to one side or the other, otherwise she will fall off. She has learned to keep her balance. Nature has several ways of staying in balance, too. The **balance of nature** refers to the condition of an ecosystem in which the producers and consumers are in a state of equilibrium—their populations are not changing significantly.

There are several ways in which we see this state of equilibrium. First, we see balance in the oxygen cycle. The amount of oxygen produced by plants is equal to the amount of oxygen used by the animals, and the amount of carbon dioxide produced by animals is equal to the amount of carbon dioxide consumed by plants. Similarly, the water and nitrogen cycles are examples of balance in nature.

We also see that in most ecosystems the number of plants is adequate for the number of primary consumers and the number of primary consumers is adequate for the number of secondary consumers, and so forth. This balance is accomplished in several different ways.

The primary way that balance is achieved is through competition for food supplies. When the food supply is low, there is more competition for a limited amount of food. The animals that eat that food must struggle to get it. Some will fail and will starve or will not be strong enough to reproduce. This will result in an increased death rate and a decreased birth rate until there is an adequate food supply for the remaining animals. Similarly, if the amount of food increases, there is less competition for the food so the death rate will go down and the birth rate will increase until equilibrium is achieved.

This is especially obvious in the predator-prey relationship. Let's look at an example. If there are too many coyotes in one area, there will not be enough

Animal Behaviors

rabbits to feed them all. The slower coyotes will not get enough food and some of them will die. Others will not be able to attract a mate and will not reproduce. This will decrease the number of coyotes. As the number of coyotes decreases, more of the rabbits will live long enough to reproduce, which will increase the number of rabbits. This process is a **predator-prey feedback loop**. When the number of prey increases the number of predators increase, but as the number of predators increase the number of prey decreases until equilibrium is reached.

This balance in nature is very important to maintaining healthy ecosystems. Many birds eat insects. If the bird population decreases, the insect population could get out of control and cause damage to food crops. We see this balance in every food chain and food web. The woodpeckers keep the wood beetle under control. There is a balance between the black-footed ferret and prairie dogs and between snowy owls and Canadian snowshoe hares. Everywhere you look, you see the balance of nature.

Equilibrium can be achieved through the predator-prey relationship, and this is a significant method by which the balance in nature is maintained today. However, this is not the only way that balance is achieved and it is not the original way that God designed nature to stay in balance. In the original creation before the Fall of man, animals did not eat each other, so God did not originally intend balance to be maintained through predator-prey relationships.

Territoriality is another way that balance can be maintained. In general, animals will respect one another's territory. You see this happening all the time, but you may not recognize what is going on. Each spring, male birds stake out a territory based on how much food is available in a given area. A bird will choose enough land to support himself, his mate, and his offspring. He will go from one edge of his territory to another singing loudly to let other males know that the area is taken. Other males will move on to unoccupied territory.

If a male cannot find an unoccupied area, he will choose not to mate that year. If all the area is taken, he will not mate until an existing pair of birds leaves or dies,

POPULATION DIAGRAMS

Choose one of the food chains you have studied. Using the animals in that food chain, draw a diagram showing what would happen to the population of each animal in the food chain if the number of primary consumers suddenly decreased. Draw a second diagram showing what would happen to the population of each animal if the number of primary consumers greatly increased. Include these diagrams in your notebook.

GROWING YOUR OWN POPULATIONS

(Optional Activity)

Purpose: To observe how an ecosystem develops its own balance of nature

Materials: cooking pot, grass, distilled water, jar, microscope, eyedropper, slides, slide cover slips, pH testing paper, "Growing an Ecosystem" worksheet

Procedure:

1. Place a handful of grass in a cooking pot with two cups of distilled water. Bring the water to a boil and boil for 3–4 minutes. This should kill all microscopic life in your ecosystem so you can establish a new ecosystem.

2. Pour the water and grass into a glass jar and place the open jar in a sunny location.

3. Each day, for seven days, test the pH of the water and record the pH level on your "Growing an Ecosystem" worksheet.

4. Each day, use an eyedropper to take a drop of water from the jar and place it on a slide. Cover the sample with a cover slip and observe the sample with a microscope. Record your observations on your worksheet. You should see different organisms appear over time.

Conclusion:

It takes about a week for a stable ecosystem to develop in a "pond" such as your grassy water in a jar. It takes about two days for decomposers such as bacteria to appear. By day 4 you should see some algae or other producers. There should be some primary consumers, such as paramecium by day 5 or 6. Finally, you may see some carnivores, such as rotifers by day 7. If the pH of the water remains in the 6 to 8 range, your ecosystem should maintain a balance between the producers and consumers.

making room for him and a new mate. This is likely part of God's original plan for population control.

Territoriality is not limited to birds. Many other types of animals also stake out territories and only breed if they can get a large enough area to support themselves and their family. Sea lions, wolves, wild cats, lemurs, and insects are just a few of the animals that defend a given territory. Birds often defend their territories through songs or elaborate shows that encourage encroaching males to back off. Many other animals, such as dogs and cats, leave scents to mark their territories. Some of these scents serve a dual purpose—to attract a mate and to define the territory.

There are other social activities that affect the populations in an area as well. Flocking has been shown to affect the number of eggs that females lay. When birds flock together, if the flock is unusually large, the females lay fewer eggs than normal. If the flock is unusually small, the females lay more eggs than normal. This helps to keep the population of the species within normal ranges.

Lions live in groups called prides and defend their territories in groups.

In general, nature will find a way to balance itself, but man can greatly upset the balance. In the early 1900s many people believed that the predators, primarily mountain lions and coyotes, were killing too many deer around the north rim of Grand Canyon. So from 1907 to 1939 hunters killed hundreds of mountain lions and over 7,000 coyotes. This had a huge impact on the deer population in that area. In 1907 there were about 4,000 deer. By 1918 there were over 40,000 and by 1923 there were nearly 100,000 deer. This huge increase in deer took a heavy toll on the plant life in the area. They were eating anything that grew. But there just was not enough food to feed that many deer. In the winters from 1923 to 1925 approximately 60,000 deer starved to death. By 1939 only about 10,000 deer were left and the plant life was still greatly damaged.

The predator-prey relationship had kept the deer population in line with the amount of food that was available. Man did not need to help control the populations; the balance of nature was already taking care of it. But when man interfered, populations got out of balance. Eventually they came back in balance, but many animals starved to death in the process. People need to be very careful about artificially changing the populations of plants or animals in stable ecosystems. ■

WHAT DID WE LEARN?

- What is meant by the balance of nature?
- Name two ways that the balance of nature is maintained in an ecosystem.
- What are two ways that animals use to stake out their territory?
- What happens if a male cannot find a territory to defend?

TAKING IT FURTHER

- What would be the likely effect on the ecosystem if a prairie dog colony was devastated by the plague?
- What would happen if animals did not respect each others' territories?
- How does the oxygen cycle demonstrate the balance of nature?
- Which methods of population control may have been present originally, and which have developed since the Fall?

ARTIFICIAL POPULATION CONTROL

God designed nature to control populations and establish balance. But many times people have changed an ecosystem for various reasons and then tried to restore balance or control the changes. People have been successful in some situations, but more often than not, people have created more problems than they have solved. Let's look at a few ways that man has tried to control the balance of nature.

Many early instances of man's interference in the balance of nature were unintentional. One of the most famous examples led to the extinction of the dodo bird (shown at right). This bird lived only on the island of Mauritius in the Indian Ocean. When people arrived on the island in the 1500s, they brought animals such as dogs, pigs, and macaques with them. These animals did not naturally live on the island and were not a part of the dodo bird food chain. Many of these animals, especially the pigs and macaques, began eating the dodo's eggs. Because there were no natural predators for the pigs and macaques, eventually these animals killed off all of the dodos and the bird is now extinct.

Man greatly upset the balance of nature and the dodo was not able to recover.

Other examples of man's interference are more purposeful, such as the killing of the mountain lions and coyotes near Grand Canyon. People thought they were helping the deer, but in the long run they upset the balance and caused suffering. Another example is the use of pesticides or insecticides in farming. Insects can cause severe damage to food crops. So farmers are always looking for ways to eliminate pests and preserve their crops. Some insecticides have been more successful than others in eliminating pests without harming the environment.

DDT is a chemical that was originally used during World War II to kill mosquitoes in an effort to

eliminate the spread of malaria and typhus. This was very successful in many areas and these diseases were greatly reduced. After the war, DDT was also used as a pesticide in farming and it was successful in eliminating many insects; however, it had many unintended consequences. DDT got into the food supply and in the water and did not easily break down. Thus when a mouse ate corn that was sprayed with DDT, the chemical stayed in its body. Although it did not kill the mouse, the DDT was spread to the hawk or eagle that ate the mouse. If the bird ate enough mice with DDT it would not be able to successfully reproduce. Thus, by controlling the insect population with chemicals, man

was inadvertently killing off hawks and eagles.

DDT was eventually banned and is no longer used as a pesticide for agriculture. However, because of its success in reducing malaria, it is being used in limited areas in Africa to help protect the people there from the disease-carrying insects. This practice is praised by some and condemned by others.

People are always researching new ways to eliminate pests without upsetting the balance of nature. One of the newer methods is to use genetically modified plants, often referred to as GMOs or genetically modified organisms. Scientists have learned how to change the DNA of some plants to make them distasteful to certain insects. This causes the insects to leave the plants alone without upsetting the food chain. Other genetically modified plants are able to grow in areas that the normal plants cannot, such as cold or very dry areas.

God has given man the task of being caretakers of His creation. We are to take care of the plants and animals that are here without hurting the environment. We must be careful to make changes that do not upset the balance of nature.

Eugene P. Odum

Father of Modern Ecology
1913–2002

In 1940 most scientists thought that the study of ecology was nothing more than observing and cataloging different plant and animal species. Ecology was considered a small part of biology. But this changed when Eugene P. Odum joined the University of Georgia as a professor of zoology and proposed that every biologist study ecology. His idea of ecology was much more than observing different species; it involved understanding interconnections within an ecosystem. Because of his revolutionary ideas, Odum is considered the father of modern ecology.

Eugene Pleasants Odum was born on September 17, 1913 in Chapel Hill, North Carolina. Odum credits his father for helping him to view the world from a holistic viewpoint; this means to look at the whole as more than just the sum of its parts—that the parts interact and work together better than they would independently.

Eugene's love of nature started at a young age, and as a teenager he wrote a weekly column about bird life for a local newspaper. He went on to receive his undergraduate and master's degrees in zoology from the University of North Carolina, and his doctorate from the University of Illinois.

Eugene married an artist named Martha Ann Huff in 1939. They spent their first year of marriage in Rensselaerville, NY where Eugene was the resident naturalist for the Edmund Niles Hyuck Preserve. He spent his time cataloging and studying the plants and animals there, while Martha spent her time painting landscapes.

In 1940 Odum began his work at the University of Georgia where he taught until his death in 2002. Together with his younger brother, Odum wrote *Fundamentals of Ecology*, an influential textbook, which was published in 1953. This was the only textbook on ecology available for the next 10 years. This book became the stimulus for the study of how plants and animals affect each other within ecosystems.

Eugene and his brother continued their research the following summer on the coral reefs in the Eniwetak Atoll in the Marshall Islands. They discovered the symbiosis between coral and algae. Their studies showed that not only does everything in nature work together, but man has an impact on ecosystems as well.

Odum's ideas of interconnectedness and balance in nature were widely publicized in his works. The impact of Eugene Odum's life is reflected in these words by the president of the University of Georgia: "We often speak about creating new knowledge through research at the University of Georgia. Eugene Odum did exactly that. No one has been able to think about the environment in the same way since he began writing about the complexities and dependencies of the relationships among organisms."

UNIT

6

ECOLOGY & CONSERVATION

MAN'S IMPACT ON THE ENVIRONMENT

Where do we fit in?

How do people fit into ecology?

Ecosystems are designed to be balanced. You just learned how populations of plants and animals are kept in balance. But man does not fit into any ecosystem. People are unique—they are different from the animals. They make their own "ecosystems." Remember back to lesson 1 when you described the different habitats you experience throughout your week? People create homes, farms, and cities that become their habitats. But this does not mean that people do not affect the plants' and animals' habitats. People can actually have a great impact on the ecosystems of the world.

Can you name some ways that people affect different ecosystems? From the time Adam and Eve were banished from the Garden of Eden, people have had to turn wild land into a home and a place to grow food. So one of the first ways that man affects ecosystems is by clearing land for homes and farms. Clearing the land and constructing buildings forces many animals to leave and find new homes. It also reduces the number of native plants, so many animals must leave to find new food sources. If people move into a forest they must chop down trees to make room for homes and crops. If people move into a grassland they have to plow under or remove the grass to make room for crops. This reduces native habitat and impacts the plants and animals in the area.

Does this mean that people should not clear the land and build on it? Not at all! God gave the earth to us for our use. Farmers not only clear the land, but use pesticides and herbicides to control the insect and plant populations on their farms. They use water to irrigate their crops. Often, they add fertilizers to the soil to increase the productivity of their crops. All of these activities have an impact on the native plants and animals, but are often necessary to ensure adequate food supplies for people.

In the past few decades, farming practices have changed to become friendlier to the environment. Many crops are planted along the contours of the land to prevent soil erosion. Crops are rotated so that different crops are grown each year. This allows the soil to naturally build back the nutrients that have been taken out and reduces the amount of fertilizers needed. Drip irrigation is used in many areas to help reduce evaporation and thus reduce the amount of water needed to grow the crops. Wind breaks have also been planted to help prevent soil erosion.

Ranching is another way that man affects the environment. Ranchers introduce non-native animals such as cattle or sheep to an area. This causes more competition for food and water and often drives out native animals. However, many animals have learned to live with the ranch animals. On some ranches the ranchers supply food for the animals, so they are not competing with the original animals for food; they still compete for space, however. Ranchers may also hunt predators to keep them from killing their animals. This impacts the whole food chain in that area.

Industry is another way that people impact ecosystems. Buildings take up space. Some industries use up resources such as water. Also, some industries put chemicals into the air that affect the plants and animals. Coal-burning power plants can add sulfur dioxide and nitrogen oxides to the air that can contribute to acid rain. Automobiles also add pollutants to the air that can affect people as well as animals. The logging industry cuts down large numbers of trees, reducing the habitat for many animals.

People also affect ecosystems with many of their recreational activities. Boating and other water activities affect the plants and animals that live in the water. Hiking can disturb the plants and animals in an area. Hunting has a definite effect on the populations of the animals being hunted and on the plants and animals in the food chain. Skiing affects mountain ecosystems. Trees are removed to make way for ski slopes, which changes the habitat for the animals that live there.

As you can see, nearly everything that people do has an impact on the ecosystems of the world and often plants and animals are hurt by reduction of their habitats or by harmful chemicals added to the air and water. Does that mean that people are bad and should do everything they can to avoid any contact with nature? Some people would have you believe that, but that is not what God intended. God created the world for man's enjoyment and then gave man the job of overseeing the use of it. We are to take care of the land and use it for God's glory. It is man's job to use the resources of the world wisely to benefit man and to glorify God. This does not mean that we have the right to abuse nature and to waste its resources. Instead, we are to recognize that the earth belongs to God and that we are to take good care of it for Him. ■

RECORDING MY IMPACT

Keep track of your activities throughout the day and record how they may impact the ecosystems around the world. Record your activities on the "How I Impact Nature" worksheet. Think about where the things you use come from, how they are made, and how those processes might affect different ecosystems. Try to think of positive impacts as well as negative impacts. What are you doing to try to minimize negative impacts?

Conservation

WHAT DID WE LEARN?

- What are some ways that farmers impact ecosystems?

- What are some ways that farmers and ranchers have changed their practices to be more friendly to the environment?

- What are some ways that industry impacts ecosystems?

TAKING IT FURTHER

- What are some ways that people can minimize their impact on nature?

- How can hunting licenses positively affect man's impact on ecosystems?

A BIBLICAL VIEW OF ECOLOGY

Should Christians be involved in ecology? Is there a Christian view of conservation? These are questions that many Christians ask. And the Bible gives us a very clear answer. In Genesis1:28 God told Adam and Eve, "Be fruitful and multiply; fill the earth and subdue it; have dominion over the fish of the sea, over the birds of the air, and over every living thing that moves on the earth." Thus man was given a job to do. He is to subdue and have dominion over the plants and animals.

In order to obey this command, Christians must recognize three things. First, man did not evolve and is not just a higher life form or another animal. Man was created in God's image. Therefore, man has a different role in ecology than plants or animals. Man is to take an active role in taking care of nature.

Second, man was commanded to be fruitful and multiply. This means man is to populate the earth. Many evolutionists claim

that the huge human population is more than the earth can bear and that people should not have children. However, this was not God's plan. God does not view man as an enemy of nature.

Third, God entrusted people to be stewards of the planet. Some people think that having dominion over nature is an excuse to exploit and use nature for our own selfish purposes. But that is not what God intended. God intends for man to administrate and care for the plants and animals. Man must be responsible for his actions and do his best to use what God has given him for his benefit, but in such a way that nature is not exploited.

Most of the ecological problems that we have today, such as pollution, damaged ecosystems, acid rain, etc. are results of human indifference, shortsightedness, selfishness, and greed. These are all moral issues. People have turned their backs on God and have used His creation for their own selfish

purposes. Many people feel that government regulations and public awareness campaigns will solve our ecological problems. While these methods have had some success, the ultimate problem is that man does not acknowledge his role as God's caretaker. To truly solve ecological problems will require people turning their hearts to God.

Although God expects us to take care of nature, many people have taken this idea to an extreme. They have become so concerned about the plants and animals that they have begun to worship nature— worshiping that which has been created, rather than worshiping the God who created it (Romans 1:20–25). This is also not what God intended. We must recognize that God is the only one worthy of our worship and that we are working on His behalf when we take care of the planet. If we keep our focus on God, we can be good caretakers of our planet.

Conservation

ENDANGERED SPECIES

Are they disappearing?

LESSON 29

What makes an animal an endangered species?

Words to know:

extinct

endangered

habitat reduction

captive breeding

By studying the fossil record, it is obvious that many species of plants and animals have become **extinct**, meaning there are no longer any of that species alive today. Many of those organisms have become extinct because of changes in climate, changing food sources, disease, and other natural causes. Many people believe that most of the dinosaurs became extinct because they could not deal well with the changes in climate after the Flood. Other plants and animals, such as the dodo bird, have become extinct because of the actions of people.

Today there are approximately 1,000 species of animals worldwide that are in danger of becoming extinct. These animals are classified as **endangered** species. In the United States alone there are approximately 700 plant species and 500 animal species that are classified as endangered. Some of these species are endangered because of the actions of people.

The main reason plants and animals become endangered is because of **habitat reduction**. As people move into new areas or clear new land for farming, many animals and plants are killed or displaced. Many animals and plants survive well in other areas and so they are relatively unaffected by man's expansion. However, some species only live in a limited area. If that area is significantly changed by man, that species may not survive. One example is the clearing of bamboo forests in China. Pandas eat bamboo and have traditionally moved from one area to another to find adequate food supplies. But as the forests are cleared, the Pandas are now limited to only a few isolated areas. When the food supplies are not adequate, the Pandas have nowhere to go. This is contributing to their declining numbers.

In addition to habitat reduction, people have introduced non-native or exotic species to various ecosystems. These new plant or animal species are often

RESEARCHING ENDANGERED SPECIES

Many of the animals you are familiar with are endangered species. Choose one or more of the animals below and write a report on it. Include this report in your notebook.

Blue Whale

Sperm Whale

Humpback Whale

Gray Wolf

Pacific Salmon

Grizzly Bear

California Condor

Snow Leopard

Giant Panda

Siberian Tiger

Black Rhinoceros

Hawaiian Monk Seal

more aggressive than the native species and can kill off or greatly reduce the native populations. This is what happened to the dodo as pigs and other animals moved in with man and ate the dodo's eggs. Another example is the zebra mussel. This tiny, shelled creature, about the size of a fingernail, is native to Russia. But in 1988 a population of zebra mussels was discovered in the Great Lakes in the United States. It is believed that these creatures were introduced to the lakes in the ballast water of ships that had been to Europe. The zebra mussels do not have many natural predators in the Great Lakes and have spread quickly to other waterways. They eat the same food as zooplankton and as they spread they are starving out many of the organisms that form the bottom of the food chains in these lakes. This affects the whole food chain. The zebra mussels are pushing many species closer to the endangered category.

Over hunting and exploitation of various plants and animals have also resulted in some species becoming endangered. Several species of whales were hunted nearly to extinction in the 1800s before most governments made it illegal to hunt them. The gray wolf has also been extensively hunted by ranchers and was once an endangered species in certain areas. Black rhinoceroses are hunted for their horns and elephants are hunted for their tusks, greatly reducing their populations. The American Bison was nearly hunted to extinction in the 1800s as well.

Pollution is also a large factor in declining populations of some species of plants and animals. When factories dump chemicals into waterways, the chemicals can have devastating effects on the wildlife in the water. Pollution released into the air can also greatly harm plants and animals. Many governments

The black rhinoceros has been hunted to near extinction for its horns.

around the world have passed laws to require companies to eliminate or greatly reduce the pollution that they release into the environment. This has helped to greatly improve the situation in many industrialized countries.

Once an animal or plant becomes endangered, it may take great efforts to change the situation and help it back toward a stable population. Many organizations have started acquiring or restoring habitats for endangered species. They have also reintroduced species to areas where they once lived in hopes that they will again thrive there. Some animals are also being bred in captivity to increase their numbers. These plans have had some success. Of all the animals listed as endangered in 1973, 68% of birds and 64% of mammals were declared to be improving and/or stable by 1994.

One of the most successful **captive breeding** programs is the breeding of the California Condor. This bird was near extinction due to hunting, lead poisoning, and poor birth rates. In 1987 all 22 of the known remaining condors were captured and taken to the San Diego Wildlife Park and the Los Angeles Zoo. There, an extensive breeding program was adopted in hopes of increasing the population. Scientists knew that if a female lost an egg, she would lay a second egg. So when the first egg was laid, the scientists took the egg away and incubated it artificially so the female would lay a second egg. This greatly improved the rate at which the population increased.

By 1991 scientists began reintroducing the California Condor into the wild. Some of these birds have reproduced in the wild, while many have not. Captive breeding continues and new birds are being released. As of May 2008 there were 332 known California Condors, 152 of these are in the wild. The breeding program for the California Condor has been the most expensive captive breeding program ever, costing over $35 million.

With the great costs associated with saving some of these endangered species, we have to ask why should we worry about saving these plants and animals? First, God made us stewards of the earth and we need to do the best we can to take care of it. In addition, many plants and animals have great value to people. Many plants and animals are used to make medicines, food, and other agricultural products. There are also many commercial uses for plants and animals and we need to ensure that

The California Condor almost went extinct.

the populations are stable. For example, logging of forests can be very beneficial as long as new trees are planted and the trees are not cut faster than they can be replaced. It is important that we do not push species to extinction. ■

WHAT DID WE LEARN?

- Name two possible natural causes of extinction of a species.
- Name three possible man-made causes of extinction of a species.
- Name three things people are doing to help endangered species.

TAKING IT FURTHER

- Why might people overhunt a particular animal?
- Can people use the land without harming endangered species?

WILDLIFE MANAGEMENT

Most people would agree that we need to do things to protect the environment and to save endangered species. However, there are no easy solutions and there are many competing ideas on how best to do this. Most nations around the world have some sort of program for providing wildlife refuges where animals cannot be hunted and habitat cannot be damaged by people. In fact, 3% of the total land areas of the world, about 2 million square miles (5 million sq. km), have been designated as protected wildlife areas.

The United Nations is one organization involved in wildlife conservation. The Food and Agriculture Organization of the United Nations (FAO) works with partner organizations around the world to not only protect wildlife, but to ensure adequate food supplies for people. Their

goal is to allow people to reap the benefits of the ecosystems today, while using them in such a way that they will be sustained for future generations as well.

In the United States there are several government organizations that help protect wildlife. The U.S. Fish and Wildlife Service is one of the largest organizations. Its goal is to "protect U.S. fish, wildlife, and plants and their habitats for the continuing benefit of the American people." They do this in many ways including enforcing wildlife laws, protecting endangered species, restoring habitat, and managing over 520 wildlife refuges. Other government agencies include the National Park Service, which manages many wildlife areas, and the Environmental Protection Agency.

In addition to government agencies, there are numerous private organizations dedicated to

preserving wildlife and protecting endangered species. Some of these organizations raise money; others raise awareness. However, many of them promote propaganda and do little more than cause panic. If you are interested in joining an organization be sure to understand its goals and methods. Some environmental groups have unbiblical goals or use questionable methods to achieve their goals.

Overall, people are much more aware of the impact of humans on the environment than they were only a century ago. There are many people trying to develop comprehensive plans for using the environment while sustaining it for future generations. Although many of these people are not Christians, they are still fulfilling the biblical mandate to subdue the earth. Christians can help lead this fight in a biblical way.

Conservation

THEODORE ROOSEVELT

1858–1919

"Keep it for your children and your children's children, and for all who come after you, as one of the great sights which every American, if he can travel at all, must see."

—Theodore Roosevelt on Grand Canyon

Who is the man that set aside more land for public protection than all the presidents before him? A homeschooler, outdoorsman, lawman, a commander of the Rough Riders, the youngest president in history—he was all of these and more. Theodore Roosevelt was born to a wealthy family in 1858, in New York. He suffered from severe asthma and had poor eye sight. For these reasons his family homeschooled him. His father encouraged him to exercise and build up his body, which he did and in the process he became a lover of the outdoors and of nature.

Roosevelt married Alice Hathaway Lee when he graduated from Harvard in 1880, at the age of 22. The following year he was elected to the New York state assembly. In 1884 his wife gave birth to a baby girl and two days later, on Valentine's Day, both his wife and his mother died. This caused him great pain. He left for the badlands of the Dakotas where he mostly isolated himself. He took up ranching and law enforcement. At this time, this part of the country was still a very rough area and

he would on occasion hunt down notorious outlaws along the Little Missouri River.

A year later, after a blizzard wiped out his herd of cattle, he headed back to New York, where he purchased a home in Oyster Bay. He kept this home until his death. The following year he ran for mayor of New York. He came in a distant third. After the election he left New York for London, where he married his childhood sweetheart Edith Kermit Carow. The couple had five children together.

In 1888 Teddy campaigned for Benjamin Harrison who was running for President. Harrison won and appointed Roosevelt to the U.S. Civil Service Commission, a post he held until 1895 when he left it to become President of the New York Board of Police commissioners. As police commissioner he made many changes, putting an end to much of the corruption in the police force. He also required the police officers to pass a physical fitness test. He saw to it that phones were installed in each police station (phones were very new at this time). And to check up on the police officers, he would sometimes walk the officer's beat late at night or in the early morning. He was also the first person to add women and Jews to the department payroll.

After working for the police force for two years, President William McKinley appointed Theodore to be Assistant Secretary of the Navy. Roosevelt loved this job and his work prepared the Navy for the coming conflict with Spain. In 1898 he resigned, and with the aid of Colonel Leonard Wood, organized the First U.S. National Cavalry, from a questionable crew of cowboys, Indians, and outlaws from the west, as well as some Ivy League boys from New York. This group later became known as the Rough Riders. They were famous for their ride up both Kettle Hill and San Juan Hill in Cuba in 1898. (In 2001 President Clinton awarded Theodore Roosevelt the Medal of Honor posthumously for this act.)

Upon his return to New York, Roosevelt ran for governor and this time he was elected. Just as when he was police commissioner, Theodore made a concerted effort to get rid of corruption in the New York government. He was too successful in his work and it is said that the political leaders in New York suggested him as a running mate for William McKinley to get him out of the way. The Vice Presidency was considered for many years as an end to political careers.

McKinley was elected with Roosevelt as his running mate. Less than a year after Roosevelt become the second youngest Vice President, he became the youngest President when McKinley was shot and died eight days later on September 14, 1901.

Roosevelt was an extremely active president. He took Cabinet members on fast-paced hikes in the gardens around D.C., horsed around with his children in the white house and on the white house lawn, kept up the boxing that he started as a boy, and read voraciously. His children were also well loved by the country.

His oldest daughter became the toast of D.C. and when friends asked him to rein her in he would answer, "I can be President of the United States, or I can control Alice. I cannot possibly do both."

In 1904 he won the election for President in a landslide victory. He continued his work to make many changes to the country. He worked hard to create what he called the "Square Deal" between business and labor. This helped to balance the power between companies and labor.

So why is a president of the United States in a book about ecology? It's because of what he did for our parks while he was president. He withdrew 235 million acres of public timberland from sale and set it aside as national forest. He created 16 national monuments, 51 wildlife refuges, and five new national parks. He set aside 800,000 acres in Arizona as Grand Canyon National Monument, which later became a national park. He also set land aside for Crater Lake in Oregon and designated the Anasazi ruins of Mesa Verde, Colorado as a National Park.

In addition to all the land he set aside for future generations to enjoy, Roosevelt also started conservation groups by inviting governors, university presidents, businessmen, and scientists to the White House to establish policies to preserve the nation's resources. As a result of his work, 41 states established conservation commissions. His work to help the West did not stop there; he also set up dam projects to irrigate farmland in 16 semi-arid states.

After serving as President for seven years, he decided not to run again but deferred to Taft. He later regretted his decision and ran again under the Reform Party's Bull Moose ticket but was unsuccessful. After WWI he was planning to run again but died in 1919 at the age of 61.

POLLUTION

What happened to clean air?

What is pollution and what can we do about it?

Words to know:

pollution

biodegradable

Challenge words:

ultraviolet radiation

chlorofluorocarbons/ CFCs

hydrochlorofluorocarbons/ HCFCs

Pollution is a problem that can affect any ecosystem. **Pollution** is the presence of any contaminant that harms the ecosystem. It could be chemicals in the water or soot in the air. Pollution can harm the plant and/or animal life in many ways.

Some pollution occurs naturally. A sandstorm in the desert can pollute an area by covering up plants with sand or filling up water holes. An erupting volcano spews tons of ash and other debris into the air. This can block sunlight and make breathing difficult. The eruption of Mount St. Helens in 1980 in Washington state shot ash 16 miles into the atmosphere where it was carried across the United States. That eruption also put tons of mud into the nearby rivers and lakes as well as destroyed thousands of trees. Wildfires are another natural source of pollution.

Although there are many natural sources of pollution, much pollution is caused by the activities of people. There are many ways that people put pollution into the environment. Pollution can come from power plants, factories, automobiles, fireplaces, controlled burns, trash, and more.

Water pollution takes a toll on all the life connected to the water. It can hurt the plants and animals that live in the water as well as the plants that grow near the water and the animals that drink the water. There are many different forms of water pollution. Chemicals often find their way into water sources from farms and factories. Also, rain washes oils and other chemicals from the streets into the storm sewers and eventually into rivers and streams.

In many undeveloped areas of the world, sewage is dumped directly into the water. This can hurt the plants and animals that live in the water as well as

Factories put chemicals, detergents, and oils into rivers.

breed diseases that harm people. It is of vital importance that sewage be treated before the water is returned to streams and rivers.

Air pollution is another problem for many ecosystems. Carbon monoxide is a poisonous gas that is a result of incomplete burning of fuels. Automobiles and power plants give off carbon monoxide. In small quantities this gas does not cause problems, but in highly populated areas the carbon monoxide levels can become dangerous. Other contaminants in the air include lead, CFCs (chemicals from air conditioners and plastics), and sulfur and nitrogen oxides. These chemicals cause various problems for people and wildlife. Smoke and other particles in the air can cause breathing problems for people and for animals, and can interfere with photosynthesis.

Most people realize that clean air is important for all life on earth. Governments have passed regulations limiting the amounts of pollutants companies and automobiles can release into the air. And new technologies have made many industries much cleaner. Because of these changes, the air today is much cleaner than it was in the 1970s. Lead is down 93%, carbon monoxide is down by 60%, and sulfur dioxide is down by 70%. We need to keep working to reduce air pollution, but great progress has already occurred.

Every week Americans produce millions of tons of garbage that goes into landfills.

Land pollution is a third area that needs to be addressed. Chemicals that are used in farming not only get into the water, but also get into the soil. Factories which produce unwanted chemicals or by-products must get rid of their waste and in the past have been known to bury it underground. Radioactive waste from nuclear power plants is a real problem. The radioactivity does not go away, so radioactive waste must be disposed of in a way that will not harm people or animals. One way that people are dealing with radioactive waste is to store it in under-

Conservation

MEASURING YOUR TRASH

One of the major sources of land pollution is trash. Every week people dump millions of tons of trash into landfills. Some of this trash will eventually decompose, meaning it is biodegradable; other items will last for hundreds of years. Reducing the amount of non-biodegradable trash will help keep landfills from filling up.

Purpose: To become aware of the amount of trash your family puts into the dump each year

Materials: rubber gloves, newspaper, bathroom scale, one week of family trash, "Our Family's Trash" worksheet

Procedure:

1. Collect all of your family's trash for one week.

2. Spread newspaper on the floor.

3. Using rubber gloves, separate the trash into five piles: metal, glass, paper, plastic, other.

4. Carefully weigh each pile and record the weight on the "Our Family's Trash" worksheet.

5. Multiply each number by 52 to calculate the yearly amount of each kind of trash your family is likely to generate. Record these numbers on your worksheet.

6. Clean up your mess and throw your trash away.

Conclusion:

Think about how much trash your family generates each year. There are millions of families around the world that are also generating trash. This can become a problem for the environment. Think of some ways your family can reduce the amount of trash it generates. One good way to reduce your trash is to recycle. Many areas have recycling programs that recycle aluminum, glass, plastics, and newspapers.

ground caves in the desert. This keeps it away from people and from most wildlife as well.

Although pollution is a real problem, in the past 40 years people have become much more aware of how their actions affect the world around them. Many programs have been implemented to help reduce or eliminate many sources of pollution. People are taking more responsibility for the pollution that they generate. There is still work to be done, but things are much better now than they were just 40 years ago. ■

WHAT DID WE LEARN?

- What is pollution?
- What are some natural sources of pollution?
- What are some sources of man-made pollution?
- What are three major areas of the environment that can become polluted?

TAKING IT FURTHER

- What are some ways that people can reduce water pollution?
- What are some ways that people can reduce air pollution?
- What are some ways that people can reduce land pollution?
- Do you think that water, air, and land are cleaner or dirtier today than they were 40 years ago?

Conservation

OZONE DEPLETION

Near the surface of the earth, most of the oxygen in the air is O_2. This means that two oxygen atoms are bonded together. This is the oxygen that people and animals need to breathe. But in the upper atmosphere, much of the oxygen has combined to form ozone which is three oxygen atoms together, O_3. We cannot breathe ozone; it is poisonous when it is down near the surface, but ozone is critical for the survival of life on earth. Ozone blocks much of the ultraviolet radiation (UV) from the sun.

We need some UV radiation to reach the surface of the earth to help warm us up, but too much UV radiation damages plant and animal tissues. Have you ever spent too much time outside on a sunny day and gotten a sunburn? The tissues of your skin were damaged by the ultraviolet radiation from the sun. Ozone in the upper atmosphere helps to limit the amount of UV radiation that reaches the surface.

In the 1970s it was discovered that substances called chlorofluorocarbons or CFCs were causing problems. CFCs are molecules that were used in air conditioning and refrigeration, aerosol sprays, and plastic foams. It is believed that the CFCs, which are very stable molecules, rise into the upper atmosphere where the UV light breaks them apart. The chlorine then bonds with the ozone, breaking off one of the oxygen atoms and turning it into O_2. The O_2 cannot protect the earth from UV radiation like ozone can. It is believed that if enough CFCs reach the upper atmosphere, enough ozone can be removed to cause problems to plants, animals, and humans. Therefore in the late 1980s CFCs were banned in most countries.

CFCs have been largely replaced with different substances called hydrochlorofluorocarbons, or HCFCs. The presence of hydrogen in the molecule makes it less stable so HCFCs react with other molecules in the atmosphere before they reach the ozone layer, thus preventing the chlorine from reaching the ozone. It is believed that the threat to the ozone layer has been slowed down and will not significantly increase. So the ozone that God created is still protecting us from UV radiation.

BLOCKING UV RADIATION

Purpose: To appreciate how ozone blocks ultraviolet radiation

Materials: clear plastic sheet protector, sunscreen lotion, newspaper, modeling clay

Procedure:

1. Completely coat one side of a clear plastic sheet protector with sunscreen lotion.

2. Make several marble-sized balls from modeling clay.

3. Place a sheet of newspaper in a sunny location.

4. Use the balls of clay to suspend the sheet protector above the newspaper by placing the balls under the edges of the sheet protector. Be sure that air can move between the sheet protector and the newspaper.

5. After several hours in the sun, remove the sheet protector. Compare the color of the newspaper that was under the sheet protector to the paper that was not under it.

Conclusion:

Newspaper is bleached to make it white. As ultraviolet rays strike the paper, the radiation causes oxygen in the air to chemically react with the paper, turning it yellow. The sunscreen blocks much of the UV radiation thus slowing the reaction with the paper. You should see a clear outline of the sheet protector where the newspaper remains whiter than the paper around it. Ozone blocks much of the UV radiation, just as the sunscreen did.

Conservation

ACID RAIN

Does it burn?

Why is acid rain harmful?

Words to know:

acid rain

buffering capacity

One of the most damaging forms of pollution in recent decades has been acid rain. Pure water does not have any acids or bases, it is neutral. But water in the atmosphere combines with some of the carbon dioxide in the atmosphere to form carbonic acid. Thus, all rainwater is slightly acidic. Most plants and animals can use slightly acidic water. The problem is that when fossil fuels such as coal, oil, and gasoline are burned, they release sulfur dioxide and nitrogen oxides. When these substances get into the air, they react with the water to form sulfuric acid and nitric acid. These acids are much stronger than carbonic acid and form what is known as **acid rain**.

When acid rain falls on an ecosystem it can damage the plant and animal life there. If lakes become too acidic the water will kill hatching fish, insects, and amphibians. This impacts the whole food chain. Acid rain in the ground reacts with other substances to release aluminum and mercury. These metals can wash into the water and do more damage to the fish and other animals that live in the water.

Acid rain also damages plants. Some plants are weakened by the acid causing them to be more easily attacked by insects and more easily blown over by the wind. Acid rain can also react with nutrients in the soil, washing them away so that plants do not have enough nutrients. This can cause plants to die. The red spruce tree is one plant that is especially sensitive to the effects of acid rain.

FUN FACT

Not all acid rain is manmade. Erupting volcanoes release large amounts of sulfur and water vapor which combine to form acid rain.

Conservation

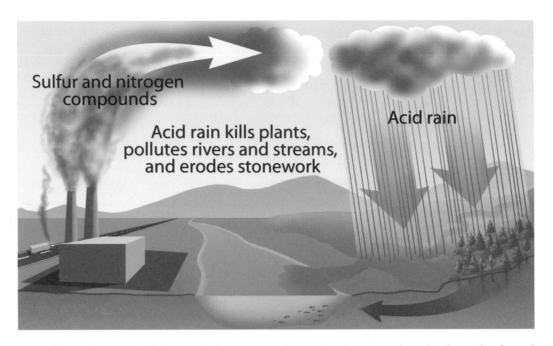

Sulfur and nitrogen compounds

Acid rain kills plants, pollutes rivers and streams, and erodes stonework

Acid rain

Although automobiles and the power plants that burn coal and oil can be found in many areas, acid rain is not a problem everywhere. Many soils have basic compounds in them which help to neutralize the acid in the rain water. This ability to neutralize acid is called the **buffering capacity** of the area. Many parts of the world have adequate buffering capacity to handle the acid rain. But areas such as

EFFECTS OF ACID RAIN

Purpose: To observe the effects of acid rain

Materials: two identical house-plants, two spray bottles, vinegar, water, "Acid Rain" worksheet

Procedure:

1. Place two houseplants in a sunny location. Label one plant with the word "water" and the other plant with "acid rain."

2. Fill one spray bottle with tap water and label it as "water." Fill a second spray bottle half full of tap water and then fill it the rest of the way with vinegar. Vinegar is an acid. Label this bottle as "acid rain."

3. Each day use the liquid in the spray bottles to water the plants. Squirt the same amount of liquid on the soil of each plant. The soil should be kept moist but not soggy.

4. Observe the plants each day for seven days. Record your observations on the "Acid Rain" worksheet.

Conclusion:

You should see a difference in the two plants after a week of watering one plant with tap water and the other with acid water. Some plants can handle acid better than others so the extent of the damage will vary with the type of plants you have.

FUN FACT

Acid rain does not necessarily have to be rain. Acid rain really refers to any acidic precipitation including snow, sleet, and hail, as well as rain.

the Adirondack and Catskill Mountains in New York have low buffering capacity so the acid rain is able to do considerable damage to ecosystems in that area.

Most countries have placed limits on the amount of sulfur dioxide and nitrogen oxides that power plants can release into the air. Thus many power plants have switched to low sulfur coal, wash their coal, and use scrubbers in their smokestacks to eliminate most of the sulfur and nitrogen compounds from the smoke they release. This has greatly reduced the amount of acid rain around the world. ■

This forest was killed by acid rain.

WHAT DID WE LEARN?

- Why is rain naturally slightly acidic?
- What is acid rain?
- What are the main causes of acid rain?
- What is buffering capacity?

TAKING IT FURTHER

- What are some ways to help reduce acid rain?
- If the buffering capacity were the same, would you expect acid rain to be more of a problem or less of a problem in areas with high population densities? Why?

ALTERNATIVE ENERGY SOURCES

There are several forms of energy that do not create acid rain. These include solar, hydroelectric, nuclear, and wind energy. Also, electric and hydrogen cars are much less likely to produce nitrogen oxides than gasoline or diesel engine cars. Choose one of these alternative energy sources and find out all you can about it. Make a presentation of what you learned and share it with your family or class. Include what you learned in your notebook. Be creative in your presentation.

Wind and solar energy are clean energy alternatives.

Conservation

GLOBAL WARMING

Is it really heating up?

Is global warming man-made?

Words to know:

greenhouse effect

global warming

deforestation

Challenge words:

non-renewable resource

Conservation

You can hardly watch the news or read a newspaper today without hearing about global warming. But you may not really understand what global warming is. Let's take a look at how the earth's temperature might change.

Energy from the sun reaches the earth. Some of the energy is reflected back into space by the atmosphere. This is because of the ozone and other molecules in the upper atmosphere. Some of the energy is absorbed by the atmosphere itself. And some of the energy reaches the surface of the earth. The energy that reaches the surface of the earth is either absorbed or reflected. Some of the reflected energy passes back through the atmosphere, but some of it is trapped by the gases in the atmosphere and some is reflected back to the surface. The gases in the atmosphere that trap energy are primarily water vapor and carbon dioxide.

The trapping of solar energy is called the **greenhouse effect**. Have you ever been in a greenhouse? The glass or plastic panels trap solar energy, keeping the temperature warmer inside the greenhouse than it is outside. The greenhouse effect on earth is very important. Without it, the average temperature on earth would be about -100°F (-73°C). But because the gases in the atmosphere trap some of the sun's energy, the average temperature on earth is a comfortable 50°F (10°C).

When the amount of energy that reaches the earth is equal to the amount of energy that is reflected back into space, the earth is in equilibrium, this means that the average temperature worldwide stays about the same. This does not mean that any particular area on earth will be exactly 50 degrees all the time. It just means that the average is staying pretty much the same.

The concern is that in the last 130 years, the average surface temperature of the earth has risen about 1.2°F, and thus the name **global warming**. Many scientists believe that this warming is primarily due to increased carbon dioxide in the atmosphere. They assert that the carbon being released by burning fossil fuels is the main cause of this global warming. They also claim that **deforestation**, the cutting of large areas of forest trees, is contributing to increasing carbon dioxide levels since plants use carbon dioxide for photosynthesis.

Some people who are concerned about global warming claim that if the current trend continues there could be severe consequences to global ecosystems. They claim that glaciers are melting at an alarming rate and that this could lead to coastal flooding and loss of habitat for polar bears. They predict that droughts will occur and deserts will expand. They also predict that more species will become extinct and diseases will spread. This is a very grim prediction of the future. So should we be alarmed about global warming? Let's take a look at some of the facts.

First, not all scientists agree that global warming is a problem. Although the media makes it sound like every scientist on the planet thinks global warming is a major problem, this is simply not true; many scientists are urging caution, not panic. It is true that the average temperature of the earth has increased by about 1.2°F in the past 130 years. It is also true that the amount of carbon dioxide in the atmosphere has increased by about 30% in the past 130 years. It is almost certain that much of the increase in carbon dioxide levels is due to the burning of fossil fuels and deforestation. However, not everyone agrees that this is a serious problem.

Some glaciers are melting. But others are growing. Many of the glaciers that are shrinking have been shrinking since the 1700s so their decrease is likely not related

THE GREENHOUSE EFFECT

Purpose: To understand how the greenhouse effect raises temperatures

Materials: two thermometers, glass jar with a lid, "The Greenhouse Effect" worksheet

Procedure:

1. Place a thermometer inside a glass jar and seal the jar.

2. Place the jar in a sunny location. Place a second thermometer next to the jar.

3. Record the initial temperature of each thermometer on "The Greenhouse Effect" worksheet.

4. Record the temperature of each thermometer every 5 minutes for 30 minutes.

Conclusion:

The radiation from the sun passes through the glass of the jar. Some of the rays are absorbed by the glass and turned to thermal energy. This traps some of the energy inside the jar and increases the temperature of the air in the jar. This is the greenhouse effect and is essentially what happens to energy passing through the atmosphere and being absorbed by the surface of the earth.

Conservation

to the recent increase in global temperatures or to increased carbon dioxide levels. On the other hand, the Briksdal glacier in Norway has been growing at a rate of 200 feet (60 m) per year. In 2005 *National Geographic* reported that glaciers in the Himalayas were shrinking. But in 2006 the same magazine reported that glaciers in the Himalayas were growing. So it is unclear the true effect that global warming is having on the glaciers overall.

Many of the dire predictions that are circulating about global warming are based on computer models of what could happen. These computer models have not been able to accurately predict what we have seen in the past 25 years, so it is unrealistic to rely on them to predict what will happen in the next 25, or even 100 years.

The Environmental Protection Agency, the organization in the United States most concerned with protecting the environment says, "Scientists are certain that human activities are changing the composition of the atmosphere, and that increasing the concentration of greenhouse gases will change the planet's climate. But they are not sure by how much it will change, at what rate it will change, or what the exact effects will be." The honest scientist will urge cautious objective research and not panic. There is simply not enough evidence to support most of the claims that you hear about global warming. Scientists continue to study other factors, including the amount of energy released by the sun, and to understand the very complex systems that control earth's climate. More time is needed to study this important issue. ■

WHAT DID WE LEARN?

- What is the greenhouse effect?
- Why is the greenhouse effect important on earth?
- What is global warming?
- What do many scientists claim are the two main causes of global warming?

TAKING IT FURTHER

- What are some ways that people might reduce the amount of carbon dioxide they are putting into the atmosphere?
- Why is it inappropriate to panic about global warming?

MORE ALTERNATIVE ENERGY SOURCES

You should be able to see by now that the use of fossil fuels, such as coal, oil, and natural gas, causes many problems. Not only are fossil fuels possibly linked to global warming, but they put many pollutants in the air, and are linked to acid rain. In addition, fossil fuels are considered **non-**renewable resources. This means that there is a limited amount of fossil fuels and they are not being replaced. This is because most fossil fuels were formed as a result of the Great Flood so they are not being formed in any large amount today.

It is important that we find alternatives to fossil fuels if we are to have reliable, clean energy in the future. Make a poster, encouraging people to use alternative energy sources. Include this poster in your notebook.

Conservation

WHAT CAN YOU DO?

How can I help?

What are the 3Rs?

Challenge words:

polymer

recycled resin

virgin resin

photodegradable

Now that you have seen some of the negative impacts that human activity can have on the environment, you might want to do something to improve the situation. In fact, because God has given people the responsibility of caring for His creation, we should do what we can to be good stewards.

Many of the issues relating to man's impact on the environment are things that have to be dealt with by adults. Children cannot develop new technologies or enforce hunting laws. But you can do a small part to reduce the amount of energy and water that you use and reduce the amount of trash that you send to the landfill.

A simple way to help you plan ways to help the environment is to think of the 3 Rs: reduce, reuse, recycle. You can reduce the amount of water you use by not running the water when you brush your teeth and by taking a short shower rather than a long bath. You can reduce the amount of energy you use by replacing regular light bulbs with compact fluorescent bulbs that use less energy while providing the same amount of light, and you can always turn off the lights when you leave a room. You can also reduce your energy usage by carpooling places with friends and neighbors or riding a bus or a bicycle.

Reusing is another way to help the environment. When you reuse something it does not go into the trash and a new one does not need to be made. This helps

FUN FACT

In 2006 Americans drank an average of 167 liters of bottled water per person. Only about 23% of these bottles were recycled. Approximately 38 billion water bottles are sent to landfills each year.

Conservation

MAKING A PLAN

Think about all the ways your family uses energy and water and think about all of the trash your family throws away. Use the ideas in this lesson and ask for ideas from your family to make a plan to help you Reduce, Reuse, and Recycle. Write out your plan on the "3 Rs of Conservation" worksheet and place it in a visible location so everyone in your family will remember to do them. Make a second copy of your plan and put it in your notebook.

reduce the impact on the environment. What things can you reuse around your house? Can you fix something that is broken instead of buying a new one? Is there someone who can use things you no longer need? Give it away instead of throwing it away.

Finally, most communities have recycling programs. You can often sign up for curbside recycling for a small fee. You can place recyclable items such as steel and aluminum cans, glass containers, newspapers, and many plastics in a special bin. Then place the bin on the curb on recycling day and the recycling company will pick them up and send them to companies that will use them to make new cans, bottles, and other items.

You can also recycle food scraps by starting a compost bin in your backyard. Fruit and vegetable peels and other food items, other than meat and dairy products, can be placed in a pile outside. Add strips of newspaper and grass clippings to the pile. Bacteria and worms will decompose these materials and turn them into compost, which can be used to fertilize your garden. Even as a kid, you can do a small part to take care of God's creation. ■

> ## FUN FACT
>
> It actually takes more energy and raw materials to make a paper cup than it does to make a Styrofoam cup.

Composting is a great way to recycle organic waste.

WHAT DID WE LEARN?

- What are the three Rs of conservation?
- List two ways you plan to do each of these things.

TAKING IT FURTHER

- Why is it important to be concerned about how humans impact the environment?

Conservation

PLASTIC RECYCLING

Plastic is something you use every day. Think about all the ways you use plastic. Your toothbrush, milk carton, refrigerator door handle, even your clothes are likely to be made from some sort of plastic. Plastic is useful because it can be made to be light and flexible, like the plastic wrap you use to cover your food or a grocery bag. Plastic can also be hard and strong like a coffee mug or door handle.

Plastic is made from petroleum, better known as oil. So in a sense it is a form of fossil fuel, although it is usually not used as fuel. The oil molecules are put together in such a way that they form long chains called polymers. Different types of plastics have different polymers. The type of plastic something is made from is usually marked on the bottom of the item with a number inside a triangle of arrows. This is a quick way to identify the type of plastic something is made from.

Many plastic items are semi-permanent parts of your life. Plastic furniture and rayon, nylon, and polyester clothes are things you are likely to keep around for a long time. Other plastics are meant to be used and thrown away, such as milk cartons or water bottles. These disposable plastic items are the ones that most people think of when they think of recycling. Products marked with a 1 or 2 on the bottom are usually picked up at curbside recycling. Plastic bags, which are a number 4, are often collected by grocery stores for recycling.

Most aluminum and glass containers that are recycled are used to make new containers. But most plastic that is recycled is made into something different. Soda bottles are often used to make carpet, T-shirts, car parts and plastic lumber. Some recycled plastic is used to make new bottles. It is too difficult and thus too expensive to recycle some types of plastic so some plastics are used as fuel for power plants. Remember, plastic is made from oil so it contains a fair amount of energy that is released as it burns.

There is a seven step process for recycling plastic. Once collected plastic reaches the recycling plant, it is first inspected and sorted. The plastic must all be the same type to be recycled together because different types of plastic melt at different temperatures and have different molecular structures. Next, the plastic is chopped into tiny flakes and washed. After this, the flakes are put into a flotation tank. Some plastic floats and other plastic sinks, so this is a second way to sort the different types of plastic.

The sorted flakes are then dried in a tumbler. After this they are melted at high temperature and pressure. The melted plastic is then pressed through a fine filter to remove any impurities. This turns the plastic into long strands. Finally, the strands are chopped into uniform sized pellets, called recycled resin. The pellets are then sold to manufacturers for various uses. In the past few years, several plastic recycling plants have closed because there has not been a good market for recycled plastic pellets. Pellets made directly from oil, called virgin resin, are often cheaper than recycled resin. However, with the recent increases in petroleum prices, this may be changing.

One of the biggest concerns about putting plastics into landfills is that they do not break down or degrade quickly. So some manufacturers are trying to make biodegradable plastic, which will break down more quickly. Biodegradable plastic is made with 5% cornstarch or vegetable oil. It is believed that bacteria in the landfills will eat the cornstarch or vegetable oil, causing the plastic to lose its structure and break down. Other plastics are photodegradable, meaning they break down when exposed to sunlight. These plastics are strong for a short period of time, but lose their strength when exposed to sunlight for a few days or weeks. Many of the 6 ring plastic holders that hold soda cans together are made from photodegradable plastics.

Today only about 5% of all plastics are being recycled. This is a very small amount compared to the total amount of plastic that is being manufactured. The EPA has a goal that 25% of all American waste should be recycled. You can do your part in helping recycle the plastics that you use.

Conservation

REVIEWING ECOSYSTEMS: FINAL PROJECT

LESSON 34

Completing your book

In this book you have learned about the world that God created. You have learned about niches and habitats, food chains, and food webs. You have learned about various ecosystems and the plants and animals that live in each one. The beauty of how everything in nature works together is a testimony to God's care for His creation.

Now is the time to finish your notebook to display all that you have learned. Make a title page and a table of contents. Decorate the cover and make it look attractive. God's beauty is everywhere so your book should reflect that beauty.

Be sure to finish all of the pages that belong in your book. Review each lesson's activity to make sure that you included each item that should be in the book. Then, if you would like to add more pages for animals or ecosystems that you are particularly interested in, feel free to do so. The goal is that someone reading your book will appreciate the wonderful creation we call earth. ■

FINAL PROJECTS

Choose one or more of the projects below to add to your notebook. Be creative and make your book a unique expression of what you have learned.

1. Make a diorama in a box of your favorite ecosystem. Take pictures and include them in the appropriate section of your notebook.

2. Cut pictures of plants and animals from magazines and make scenes of appropriate ecosystems. Only include plants and animals that are likely to share a particular ecosystem. Add your scenes to the appropriate sections of your notebook.

3. Paint a picture of how you imagine the Garden of Eden might have looked. Add your painting to the first section of your notebook.

4. Make a chapter page for each section of your notebook.

5. Take photographs of plants and animals from as many different ecosystems as you can visit. Add them to your notebook.

Conservation

CONCLUSION

Appreciating our beautiful but cursed world

LESSON

35

Thank God for this amazing planet.

W hen God created the world he pronounced it "very good" (Genesis 1:31). It was a perfect world without death. But man sinned and God cursed the earth. This changed the way the world works. Death is now the rule and thorns and weeds grow rampant. Romans 8:22 tells us that the Curse did not just change life for men—all of nature was affected.

Even with the Curse, creation still declares the glory of God (see Psalm 19:1 and Romans 1:20–21). When we look at the diversity among all living things, the amazing interactions among plants and animals, and the interdependence of different species, we see the marks of design—they are not an accident. Your study of ecosystems should have helped to open your eyes to the wonder of God's creation.

God is concerned about everything in His creation. In Matthew 6:28–29 we read, "And why do you worry about clothes? See how the lilies of the field grow. They do not labor or spin. Yet I tell you that not even Solomon in all his splendor was dressed like one of these." Matthew 10:29 says, "Are not two sparrows sold for a copper coin? And not one of them falls to the ground apart from your Father's will." If God cares for the smallest animal and the plants of the field, we should care for them, too. We are to fulfill the commission given to Adam and Eve to take care of every living thing.

Most importantly, Matthew 10:31 goes on to say, "Do not fear therefore; you are of more value than many sparrows." Man is infinitely more valuable to God than any animal or plant He created. That is why Christ came to die for us. So we need to first dedicate ourselves to God, and then we can care for His creation as He intended. ■

 ## A POEM

Write a poem expressing your love for the Creator and the beauty of His creation. Include your poem as the final entry in your Ecosystems Notebook.

Conservation

LESSON 35 PROPERTIES OF ECOSYSTEMS · 139

GLOSSARY

Abiotic Nonliving

Acid rain Precipitation that has a higher than normal acid level

Adaptation Physical trait or behavior due to inherited characteristics that gives an organism the ability to survive in a given environment

Algae bloom Sudden rapid growth of algae

Alpine tundra Tundra on high mountains

Antarctic tundra Tundra below the Antarctic Circle

Arboreal Living life primarily in trees

Arctic tundra Tundra above the Arctic Circle

Atoll Coral reef formed around a sunken volcano

Bactrian camel Two-humped camel

Balance of nature Condition in which the producers and consumers are in equilibrium

Barrier reef Coral reef formed away from the shore

Beach Shore where the ocean meets the land

Benthos Plants and animals that live on the ocean floor

Biodegradable Able to be decomposed by natural means

Biome Many connected ecosystems that share a similar climate

Biosphere Area of the earth containing life

Biotic Living

Buffering capacity Ability of the soil to neutralize acid

Camouflage How an animal blends in with its surroundings

Canopy Roof of forest, formed by tops of mature trees

Captive breeding Breeding of endangered species in captivity

Carnivore Organism that eats only animals

Cave Cavern in a mountain or underground

Chaparral Area on hot dry mountain slopes with dense shrubbery

Chemosynthesis Conversion of chemicals into food

Climate The general or average weather conditions of a certain region

Cold desert Desert with daytime temperatures below freezing in the winter

Commensalism Relationship in which one species benefits and the other is unaffected

Community All the populations living together in a given area

Competition Relationship in which two species compete for scarce resources; can be harmful to both species

Coniferous forest/Boreal forest/Taiga Ecosystem dominated by coniferous trees

Coniferous tree Tree with needle-like leaves that bear seeds in cones

Consumer Organism which obtains energy by eating other organisms

Coral reef Formation built from exoskeletons of coral polyps

Deciduous forest Ecosystem dominated by deciduous trees

Deciduous tree Tree with broad, flat leaves that are shed in autumn

Decomposer Organism that breaks down dead plants and animals into simpler elements

Decomposition The act of breaking down dead tissues into simpler elements

Deforestation Cutting of large numbers of trees without replacing them

Desert Area that receives less than 10 inches of rain per year

Dromedary camel   One-humped camel

Dynamic equilibrium   The amount of debris deposited is equal to the amount removed

Ecology   Study of the interaction of the environment and living things

Ecosystem   Community of living things and the environment in which they live

Emergent layer   Top layer of a forest

Endangered   A species is in danger of becoming extinct

Ephemeral   Plant with an accelerated life cycle

Epiphyte   A plant that grows on another plant without harming it

Estivation   Summer sleep in which the animal's metabolism is very slow

Estuary   Ecosystem where fresh water flows into the ocean

Evergreen tree   Tree with needle-like leaves that are not shed in autumn

Extinct   There are no living specimens of a particular species

Fauna   Animals in an ecosystem

Floor   Ground layer of forest

Flora   Plants in an ecosystem

Food chain   Diagram of the flow of energy from one organism to another

Food web   Diagram showing the interconnection of the food chains within an ecosystem

Forest   Ecosystem dominated by trees

Fringing reef   Coral reef attached to land

Global warming   Increase in the average surface temperature of the earth

Grassland   Ecosystem dominated by grass with few trees or shrubs

Greenhouse effect   The warming of the earth due to trapped radiation

Guano   Bat or bird droppings

Habitat reduction   Destruction or elimination of natural habitat

Habitat   The environment in which an organism lives

Herb layer   Layer of forest containing grass, flowers, and other small plants

Herbivore   Organism that eats only plants

Hibernation   Winter sleep in which the animal's metabolism is very slow

Hot desert   Desert that does not experience freezing temperatures

Inter-tidal zone   The part of the shore that is covered with water at high tide and uncovered at low tide

Lake   Large body of freshwater

Law of conservation of mass   Mass/matter cannot be created or destroyed by any natural means; it can only change form

Mangrove forest   Estuary dominated by mangrove trees

Midnight/Aphotic zone   Layer of water that sunlight is unable to penetrate

Migration   Moving from one area to another for a particular season

Mirage   An optical illusion that reflects the sky onto the ground making it appear as water

Mutualism   Relationship in which both species benefit

Natural selection/Survival of the fittest   Ability of an organism to survive better than others of its kind because of a particular characteristic

Nekton   Animals that freely move throughout the ocean

Neutralism   Relationship in which two species do not significantly benefit nor harm one another

Niche   Role of an organism within its environment

Nocturnal   Active at night

Northern polar region   Area of earth north of the Arctic Circle

Northern temperate zone   Area of earth between Tropic of Cancer and Arctic Circle

Oasis   An area in the desert watered by a spring

Omnivore   Organism that eats both plants and animals

Overturn   Rapid exchange of cold and warm water regions within a lake

Oxygen cycle   Process through which oxygen is recycled

Pampas Grasslands of South America

Parasitism Relationship in which one species benefits and the other is harmed

Permafrost Layer of ground that does not defrost even in summer

Photosynthesis Chemical reaction in which water and carbon dioxide are changed into glucose and oxygen using sunlight

Phytoplankton Microscopic aquatic organisms that perform photosynthesis

Plankton Plants and animals that move with the ocean currents

Pollution Any contaminant that harms an ecosystem

Pond Lake that is too shallow to have an aphotic zone

Population Number of a species in a given area

Prairie Grassland of North America

Predator Animal that hunts other animals

Prey Animal that is hunted by other animals

Predator-prey feedback Process in which a change in population among the prey produces a change in population among the predators and vise-versa

Producer Organism which produces its own food

Respiration Chemical reaction in which glucose and oxygen are changed into water and carbon dioxide

Riparian zone Land along the banks of a river or stream

River/Stream Freshwater that is flowing

Salt marsh Estuary dominated by rushes

Salt meadow Estuary dominated by sea grass

Savannah Grassland of Africa

Scavenger Organism that eats dead plants or animals

Semi-arid Climate with more rain than a desert but less rain than temperate areas (usually 10–20 inches of rain per year)

Shrub layer Layer of forest containing shrubs and other short plants

Snow line Altitude above which the snow does not completely melt each year

Southern polar region Area of the earth south of the Antarctic Circle

Southern temperate zone Area of earth between Tropic of Capricorn and Antarctic Circle

Steppe Grassland of Europe and Asia

Stomata Tiny holes in leaves for exchange of gases and releasing water

Succulent Plants with fleshy stems for storing water

Sunlit/Euphotic zone Layer of water that sunlight is able to penetrate

Symbiosis Close relationship between two different species

Territoriality An animal's defense of its territory for breeding or other purposes

Tide pool Area along shore that fills with water during high tide

Timberline Altitude above which no trees can grow

Transpiration The release of water from leaves

Tributary Smaller stream or river that flows into a larger stream or river

Troglobites Animals that spend their entire lives in caves

Troglophiles Animals that like to live in caves but can be found living outside caves as well

Trogloxenes Animals that visit caves but don't spend their whole lives there

Tropical rainforest Forest in tropical region receiving more than 80 inches of rain per year

Tropical zone Area of earth between Tropic of Cancer and Tropic of Capricorn

Tundra Treeless area with long cold winters and cool summers

Twilight/Disphotic zone Layer of water that only a small amount of sunlight is able to penetrate

Understory Layer consisting of immature trees and shorter species

Water cycle Process through which water is recycled

Zooplankton Microscopic aquatic consumers

CHALLENGE GLOSSARY

Adaptive radiation   Development of several species from one common ancestral kind

Animal courtship   Animal behaviors performed to attract a mate

Biogeographic realms/Ecozones   Large areas of land separated by natural barriers

Bioluminescence   An organism's ability to produce its own light

Cambium   Area inside a tree where new bark and wood cells are produced

Carrying capacity   Maximum population an area can support

Chlorofluorocarbons/CFCs   Molecules used in refrigeration and plastics that degrade ozone

Climax ecosystem   Final, stable ecosystem

Coral bleaching   Condition in which coral expels its symbiotic algae

Dormant   An inactive, non-growing state

Dune system   Ecosystem that develops as you move inland from the shore

Echolocation   Use of high pitched sound waves to detect objects

Ecotone   Transitional area between two different ecosystems

Fire cue   Condition caused by fire which triggers seed germination

Genetically modified organism/GMO   An organism whose DNA has been intentionally modified by man to produce a particular trait

Heartwood   Center of tree; dead wood cells which provide support and strength

Hyrdorchlorofluorocarbons/HCFCs   Molecules used to replace CFCs in many applications

Maritime forest   Area inland from the shore containing shrubs and trees

Nitrogen cycle   Process through which nitrogen is recycled

Non-renewable resources   Natural resources that are not being replaced

Outer bark   Protective outer layer of a tree trunk or branch

Papillae   Tiny projections

Phloem/Inner bark   Carries food down from leaves

Photodegradable   Able to be decomposed by sunlight

Pioneer plants   First plants to move into an area after a drastic change

Polymer   Very long chain of molecules used to form plastics and other materials

Primary dune   Area along the beach that is dominated by grass

Recycled resin   Plastic pellets made from recycled plastic

Secondary dune   Area inland from the primary dune that is covered with shrubs and grass

Succession   Change over time from one ecosystem to another

Ultraviolet radiation/UV radiation   Energy rays from the sun that can cause damage to plant and animal tissues

Virgin resin   Plastic pellets made directly from oil

Watershed   All the land drained by a particular river or body of water

Xylem/Sapwood   Carries water and nutrients from roots to the rest of the tree

INDEX